NEW TESTAMENT CHRISTIANS

The Seven Secrets of the Wonderfully Happy Converts at Pentecost

WHAT KIND of Christian are you going to be? Perhaps you did not even know that there could be more than one kind of Christian, but there certainly can! You may be a happy, joyful Christian, rejoicing in the Lord always, as we are commanded to do (Phil. 4:4); or you can be like so many others, happy only part of the time.

You may be the kind of Christian who *knows* that he is saved, never doubts it because he knows just how he was saved and that God keeps His promises. Or you may be the kind of Christian who frequently doubts his salvation and wonders if God has not forsaken him.

You may be the kind of Christian who has regular daily victory over sin, the kind of Christian who is able to overcome daily temptations and, though he will know that he is naturally weak and frail and sinful, yet has such daily cleansing and daily power to turn away from known sin that on the whole his life is one grand victory! Or you may be the kind of Christian who, though truly converted and truly loving the Lord Jesus in his heart and knowing he has trusted Christ for salvation, is nevertheless constantly defeated, often falling into sin or having habits that he seems unable to break. You see, a Christian may be victorious or defeated.

A Christian may find great joy in the Bible and read it daily with increasing profit and help and enjoyment. Or a Christian may find the Bible dull, may feel himself more or less unable to master the Word of God and to live by its precepts because he is not a mature and victorious Christian. I know Christians like that, don't you?

A Christian may be a soul winner. Certainly that is the highest aim of our Saviour for every Christian. He may day by day have the power of the Holy Spirit upon him so that he will know what to say to sinners and may find that the blessed Holy Spirit takes his testimony and warnings and uses them powerfully in turning sinners to Christ. Or a Christian may go along from the day of his salvation and never win a soul, and meet God empty handed at the judgment seat of Christ! What a sad thing to be one of the branches of Christ, the Vine, but to bear no fruit! What a sad thing to be saved, as Lot was down in Sodom, but to have one's family and kinspeople and neighbors destroyed and sent to Hell because one did not have the power to win them!

The Defeated, Carnal Christians at Corinth

The Word of God recognizes that there are these two kinds of Christians—the victorious and the defeated, the happy and the sad, the prosperous and the unprosperous, the soul winners and the unfruitful. In writing to the church at Corinth the Apostle Paul was inspired to say:

"And I, brethren, could not speak unto you as unto spiritual, but as unto carnal, even as unto babes in Christ. I have fed you with milk, and not with meat: for hitherto ye were not able to bear it, neither yet now are ye able. For ye are yet carnal: for whereas there is among you envying, and strife, and divisions, are ye not carnal, and walk as men? For while one saith, I am of Paul; and another, I am of Apollos; are ye not carnal?"—I Cor. 3:1-4.

You see, it was a sad fact that many of these new converts at Corinth were still only babes in Christ, though they had been saved some time before. They were still weak and were not able to eat the strong meat of the Word of God, but had to be fed upon milk. They were "carnal" and not "spiritual." There were only baby Christians. They could not have the regular strong food that Christians ought to be able to enjoy. They had divisions and strifes. They were envious. They had a tendency to follow human leaders without having the spiritual wisdom to follow Christ, through Christ's men. And elsewhere in this epistle we find that many of these Christians lived defeated lives. Some of them even came drunk to the Lord's table. One man was living in shameful sin with his stepmother, and others in the church took his part. So there were quarrels. And though Paul writes to these as really born-again Christians, yet he frankly charges that many of them were carnal, defeated, unspiritual Christians.

But the Bible, thank God, shows us just how to be grown-up Christians instead of babies. The Bible shows us how to be happy Christians instead of sad and despondent ones. The Bible shows us how to be fruitful soul winners so that we will not come empty handed to meet our Saviour and be ashamed before Him. The Bible shows us how we may *know*, know all the time, that we are saved and kept saved by the power of God. The Bible shows us how we may have our prayers answered regularly, daily. And in this little book I will earnestly try to show you God's seven secrets of a happy, prosperous Christian life.

Would you like to be happy all the time, never defeated, never finding yourself estranged from God? Would you like to know how to have your prayers answered every day? Would you like to know how to have the power of the Holy Spirit upon you so you can win souls regularly right on through your life? Would you like to be close enough to God all the time that you could have the leading of the Holy Spirit to know what to do? Well, that is a wonderful thing and I will show you plainly by the Bible just how you may live in that blessed state of a spiritual Christian, just how you can live a happy, victorious, prosperous Christian life all the time!

The Wonderful Example of the Converts Saved at Pentecost

In the book of Acts we have a marvelous example of New Testament Christians who lived happy and prosperous and victorious lives; who got their prayers answered, who won their loved ones to Christ, who knew they were saved, who continued on the high plane of daily revival blessing all the time! I refer to the Christians at Jerusalem who were converted at the revival of Pentecost. Since this little book will fall into the hands of many new converts, I want to use these Pentecostal converts as an example for you. These converts of the greatest revival in the history of Christianity went on to live for God so boldly and happily that we will do well to study from the Word of God just how they did it. What were the secrets of their wonderfully prosperous and happy Christian lives?

That question is answered in Acts 2:41-47. Let us read this Scripture telling of those who were saved at Pentecost and of what followed in their lives, and learn their seven secrets of a happy, prosperous Christian life.

"Then they that gladly received his word were baptized: and the same day there were added unto them about three thousand souls. And they continued stedfastly in the apostles' doctrine and fellowship, and in breaking of bread, and in prayers. And fear came upon every soul: and many wonders and signs were done by the apostles. And all that believed were together, and had all things common; And sold their possessions and goods, and parted them to all men, as every man had need. And they, continuing daily with one accord in the temple, and breaking bread from house to house, did eat their meat with gladness and singleness of heart, praising God, and having favour with all the people. And the Lord added to the church daily such as should be saved."—Acts 2:41-47.

How my heart is thrilled as I read this passage and see how happy were these new converts, how joyful was their fellowship! They ate their meat "with gladness and singleness of heart, praising God." And the Lord kept on saving souls through their earnest, Spirit-empowered pleading and their glad testimony!

But as we read the passage we note that there did not come a great crisis by which they were instantly made holy, sinless, with all the natural temptations and weaknesses of the human flesh taken away. No, if we study the Scripture here carefully we will find instead that there were certain rules these new converts followed and by so doing they continued in the joy and power of the blessed revival in which they were converted. Here we find the seven secrets of a happy Christian life.

You will be surprised, perhaps, when I say that all these seven secrets are shown in this passage. But when I call them to your attention, you will recognize them, I am sure.

FIRST SECRET: These converts had the assurance of salvation based upon the plain Word of God. *"Then they that gladly received his word were baptized. . . ."* (vs. 41).

SECOND SECRET: The new converts were baptized, thus publicly confessing Christ, each one thus publicly renouncing and counting dead and burying the old sinner that each had been; and publicly rising from the waters of baptism to live a resurrected life, in the power of Christ. "Then they . . . were baptized" (vs. 41).

THIRD SECRET: The new converts were added to the local assembly of Christians; they joined the church. "And the same day there were added unto them about three thousand souls" (vs. 41). "And they continued stedfastly in . . . fellowship, and in breaking of bread . . ." (vs. 42).

FOURTH SECRET: They continued stedfastly in the apostles' doctrine, that is, in the Word of God, learning and following and meditating in the teachings of the Bible, which is the apostles' doctrine written down. "And they continued stedfastly in the apostles' doctrine . . ." (vs. 42).

FIFTH SECRET: They continued constantly in prayer. "And they continued stedfastly . . . in prayers" (vs. 42).

SIXTH SECRET: They put God first in their possessions, counted all they had as belonging to God and used possessions to please Him. "And all that believed were together, and had all things common; and sold their possessions and goods, and parted them to all men, as every man had need" (vss. 44, 45).

SEVENTH SECRET: They were so joyful, so filled with the Spirit, so constant in their pleading and their testimony for God that they won souls daily. And the church, instead of receiving converts once a year, at Easter, or once a month, received the new converts daily! "And the Lord added to the church daily such as should be saved" (vs. 47).

Here we have the principles by which these new converts lived. We have their seven secrets of a happy, prosperous Christian life. Oh, if the converts in every revival would set out to live after these same principles, live so joyfully and victoriously and fruitfully, how soon we would see multiplied thousands of souls saved! Well, dear reader, you yourself may learn here and now to live such a happy, victorious and prosperous Christian life by following the example of the Christians at Jerusalem who were converted in the revival at Pentecost. I know these principles work because God has graciously worked them in my own life. And I have seen them demonstrated in the lives of thousands of others. So take most seriously these lessons, and I can assure you that you will be a joyful, victorious Christian, having your prayers answered, winning souls to the Lord and being wonderfully prospered in all good things.

CHAPTER I

ASSURANCE OF SALVATION BY THE WORD

First Secret of Christian Happiness and Success

THE FIRST RULE for a happy and successful Christian life is to *know* that you are saved! This is the very foundation of Christian happiness and Christian usefulness and spiritual properity.

Jesus said, "Rejoice, because your names are written in heaven" (Luke 10:20). And how can you have that rejoicing if you do not know whether or not your name is written in Heaven?

How can you have confidence when you come to pray if you do not even know that you are God's child? If you do not know that the first prayer that you ever prayed— the prayer for forgiveness and salvation—has been answered, how can you have any confidence to pray for the salvation of others?

If you do not know that you yourself were saved, and if you have not understood the Word of God clearly enough to convince yourself of your salvation, then how could you make the same road to salvation clear to others? D. L. Moody said after many years of experience that he had never seen a single successful soul winner who was not sure about his own salvation.

1. Only Those Who Gladly Received the Word Were Baptized

One can see how wise was Spirit-filled Peter and the other apostles to demand that those who came for baptism should gladly receive the Word of God and base on that Word their assurance of salvation. After Peter had preached and made clear the plan of salvation, we are told, "Then *they that gladly received his word* were baptized" (Acts 2:41).

Who were baptized? Let us imagine the scene. The power of God has fallen in a wonderful way. Multitudes have turned to Christ, this day of Pentecost when the hundred and twenty who have been waiting in the upper room for ten days "were all filled with the Holy Ghost." Sinners, pricked in their hearts by Peter's sermon, had been plainly told that they should repent and then should be baptized as an outward declaration of that repentance, and were promised not only that they should be saved but that they should also have, like these others at Pentecost, "the gift of the Holy Ghost." They had been told clearly how Christ had been crucified for them and, from the text in Joel 2:32, they had had it preached to them that "whosoever shall call on the name of the Lord shall be saved" (Acts 2:21). Their baptism, then, was to be strictly a sign that they believed their sins were remitted when they repented, calling upon Christ for salvation. I can imagine that a man steps up and says, "Peter, I want to be baptized, too, as a Christian."

"But are you saved? Are your sins forgiven? Why do you claim that your sins are forgiven, and on what basis do you call yourself a child of God?" I imagine that Peter asked.

To this I can imagine that the new convert plainly says, "I have just heard that God raised Jesus Christ from the dead, proving that He is the Christ of the Old Testament. I believe, then, that He died for my sins. According to the Word of God, 'whosoever shall call on the name of the Lord shall be saved.' My heart has called upon Him, trusted in Him. My heart has turned from its sin, depending on Jesus. I believe that He has forgiven me and saved me because the Word of God you quoted to us from Joel says that 'whosoever shall call on the name of the Lord shall be saved,' and I have called upon Him. Peter, I believe the Word you have preached and I am claiming to be a child of God and to have a right to be baptized on the basis of the Word of God."

The crowd of Christians smile and thank God for a sinner saved, and the apostles nod their heads in united approval. "Yes! He is ready to be baptized. He has gladly received the Word of God, has trusted Christ for his salvation and is depending upon God's Word that he is saved. His assurance is based on what God has plainly promised." And so the man was approved for baptism.

But I imagine that some other man comes and says, "I, too, want to be baptized. I want to be a Christian. In fact, I call myself a Christian already and I think I ought to be baptized as others are being baptized."

"And on what basis do you claim that your sins are forgiven and that you are a child of God?" I imagine that the Apostle John may have asked him. "I'm so glad that you want to be a child of God and I trust that you are. Now if you have really been saved you ought to be baptized, but how do you know that you are saved?"

Let us imagine that this man says, "I've heard the plain preaching of Peter and I am pricked in my heart. My conscience accuses me of my sins. Therefore, I want to do better. I have resolved never to be drunk any more, never to lie or steal. I want to serve God and win His approval. I feel sure that if I live right and hold out faithful He will receive me. Therefore, I want to be in the church with God's people, to live with them and among them, and I hope to hold out faithful to the end and prove myself a Christian."

Here is a man who wants to do right, wants to be saved. But either he is not saved or he, while trusting in his heart, does not have the assurance of salvation based upon the plain Word of God. His assurance may be a fleeting assurance that will leave at the first temptation or persecution. He may "feel" all right now, but what about when he comes into temptation or neglects to pray, or when he finds it difficult to live as a Christian ought? So I imagine that the Apostle John, the Apostle Peter and others would sadly shake their heads and say, "No, no, my friend! Before you are baptized we feel that you ought to have assurance based upon the Word of God. We are baptizing only those who gladly receive God's Word on this matter and base their hope upon God's Word." So the man would either be instructed further and taught to base his assurance upon the Word of God, or he would be denied baptism until that matter was made clear. The man might be an unsaved man depending on his works. Or he might be a really born-again Christian but poorly instructed and with a cloudy understanding of the way of salvation. But at Pentecost, we are told, only those were baptized who gladly received the Word as it was preached by the other Christians, particularly by Peter in the public message.

2. Can One Absolutely Know He Is Saved?

Years ago I heard a good woman say to her pastor in a public prayer meeting: "But, Brother Pastor, it seems to me it would be very presumptuous for me to say that I *know* I am saved. I can say that I have a hope of salvation but I know that I am unworthy. I could say that I intend to do my part and trust that the Lord will forgive me and take me to Heaven. But would it not be presumptuous for me to say that I *know I* am good enough to go to Heaven?"

To this the pastor very wisely replied, "None of us is good enough for Heaven in our own works. Every one of us is a poor Hell-deserving sinner. The only ones who can ever go to Heaven are sinners who are saved by God's undeserved mercy and grace, sinners cleansed by the blood of Christ. So," he said, "nobody in the world has any right to count on his goodness, on his character, on his righteousness to get him to Heaven.

"But, on the other hand," the pastor continued, "if I have come to Christ and trusted in His atoning blood, and if the Word of God gives me clear assurance that 'he that believeth on the Son hath everlasting life' (John 3:36), and 'he that believeth on him is not condemned' (John 3:18), and that 'whosoever shall call on the name of the Lord shall be saved' (Acts 2:21), then I would not be presumptuous to claim what God has said is true. I would be making Him a liar and doubting Him if I did not claim what He said was true. So when I know I have trusted in Jesus Christ and not in myself; when I know that I have depended on what Jesus has done for me and what He has promised that He would do for me, then it is not presumption but is an honest faith that can say, 'I know I am saved!'"

But does the Bible clearly say, in so many words, that we can *know* we are saved? Yes, thank God, it does! In I John 5:13 are these blessed words: "These things have I written unto you that believe on the name of the Son of God; that ye may know that ye have eternal life, and that ye may believe on the name of the Son of God." A part of the Bible is written, we are told, for the express purpose "that ye may know that ye have eternal life . . ."

Years ago I was preaching in a tent revival campaign in San Antonio, Texas. Two lovely girls sixteen and eighteen years of age came under the tent one night just before the song service began. I gave each of them a song book and then said to the older girl, "Are you a Christian? Have you been saved?"

She looked at me with an innocent face and said respectfully, "Yes, I think I am a Christian. Of course, I do not know. I don't think you *can* know. But I do the best I know how and I think I can say that I am a Christian. Of course, nobody can know for sure whether or not he is saved."

"Oh yes, you *can* know," I said. "And you ought to make sure and know that you are saved."

"But I do not think that you *can* know," she said.

"Well," I said, "let us not argue about it. Suppose I find it in the Bible that you can know that you are saved. Would you believe it then?" I asked.

"Yes, of course I will believe it if it is in the Bible. But I do not believe it is there. I do not believe that one can know that he is saved."

I got my Bible and turned to this wonderful passage in I John 5:13, and holding the Bible before her we read it together: "These things have I written unto you that believe on the name of the Son of God; that ye may know that ye have eternal life, and that ye may believe on the name of the Son of God."

"You see," I said, "you *can* know that you are saved. Here in the Bible is a portion of Scripture that was written expressly so you can know that you are saved."

I saw the tears start up in her eyes, and then she looked at me and said very softly and with deep emotion, "Yes! One can know!"

"Now read the rest of the verse carefully," I said. "How does one get to be a child of God so he can know it?"

She read the verse again: "These things have I written unto you *that believe* on the name of the Son of God; that ye may know that ye have eternal life, AND THAT YE MAY BELIEVE ON THE NAME OF THE SON OF GOD."

"I see it now! One who believes in Christ and depends on Christ has a right to know that he has eternal life!" she said. And then we bowed our heads and asked the Lord Jesus to help her trust Him right there. And she did trust Him. She took my hand earnestly as a sign that there and then she would claim Him as Saviour and went away *knowing* that she had everlasting life. And her sixteen-year-old sister likewise trusted Christ and on the basis of this plain Word of God knew that she had everlasting life.

Oh yes, then, one can *know* that he is saved.

There are a number of similar passages in the Bible which clearly say that one can know he is saved. For example, in I John 5:19 we are told: "And we *know* that we are of God, and the whole world lieth in wickedness."

Again I John 3:14 says, "We *know* that we have passed from death unto life, because we love the brethren . . ."

Again in I John 2:3 we are told, "And hereby we do know that we know him, if we keep his commandments."

3. But This Perfect Assurance of Salvation Is Not Automatic; One Can Be Truly Converted and Yet Have Doubts, Not Perfect Assurance

Some people think that if anything so wonderful as forgiveness of sins and the salvation of the soul has happened to a person, that he could never doubt it. Some people believe that when one is saved he automatically knows and can never doubt his salvation. But that position is not supported by the Word of God. Actually, a Christian *can* know beyond any doubt that he is saved, and every Christian *ought* to know beyond any doubt that he is saved; but many people, in fact, do not know it. That assurance has to come by an understanding of the Word of God.

It is true that many people have such a sweet assurance and peace and joy at the time of their turning to Christ that they are happy and have a sweet assurance, for the time being, based upon the "experience." They say, "I was there when it happened and I ought to know!" Some tell how they felt as light as a feather. Others tell how they saw a bright light shining from Heaven. Others tell how they praised God aloud and felt the glory of the Lord in their souls. Some tell how they were instantly changed and how old habits dropped away and that things they once hated they now loved and what they once loved they now hated. Some people, after they have trusted in Christ, have an assurance that is based upon their feelings, their emotions, upon their experiences. But, alas, that kind of assurance does not always last! They feel wonderful for the present, but the time comes when they lose their sense of God's nearness. Perhaps through lack of prayer, or lack of meditation upon the Word of God, or through some sin or some neglect, they lose the sense of God's constant presence and lose the sense of His forgiveness. Immediately such people are prone to believe that they have lost their salvation. Or, when the feelings of joy and happiness disappear, then one who depends upon his feelings may think, "I suppose I was mistaken. Probably I was never saved or I would not feel like this and I would not fall into the sins that trap me now." Or one who depends on his feelings may, after a great struggle with conscience and trying again and again to feel as he once felt, decide that he has committed the unpardonable sin, that the Spirit of God has left him forever because of some real or fancied sin. Oh, I tell you it is an uncomfortable business trying to depend upon one's feelings for the assurance of salvation!

How well I know about this! When I was nine years old I trusted Christ as my Saviour. It was after a good sermon by a godly pastor in Gainesville, Texas. He preached upon the parable of the prodigal son and told us how any poor sinner who would turn to the Lord would receive a glad welcome and forgiveness and peace, and that, like the prodigal son, we would receive all these blessings without money and without price, wholly undeserving. Then he asked those who would take Christ as Saviour and trust Him, turning in their hearts to the Father's house for mercy and forgiveness, to come forward. I slid off the pew, walked down the aisle and took the pastor's hand to claim Christ as my Saviour. They did not take time to teach me any of the Word of God. Perhaps they thought I was too young. I went home so happy that day and asked my father if it would be all right for me to join the church and be baptized since I was now a Christian. He said, "Well, Son, when you are old enough to know you are a sinner and honestly repent of your sins and be regenerated, then it will be time enough to join the church."

I sat stricken and silent before my father. I did not know what all those big words meant; *repentance* and *regeneration*

and more. I simply knew my father did not think I was
saved! Well, I thought, my father was the wisest man in the
world and a preacher, besides; and if he thought I was not
saved, I supposed I was not. Sadly I gave up the idea of
joining the church and hoped the time would soon come when
I would be old enough to be saved so my father would know
that I was saved.

The next morning on the way to school I stopped under a
willow tree down on Pecan Creek and prayed. I asked God
to help me to be a good boy and asked Him to save other
people, since my father thought I was too young to be saved.

I wish I could tell you all the sadness and disappointment
of the next three years. I often prayed. We moved out to a
ranch in west Texas and then to a little cow town. The
company was not always the best. My mother had gone to
Heaven, and I was a motherless boy. I did not get much
instruction in the Word of God. I got no assurance about
salvation. Again and again I prayed for God to save me.
Once I asked a godly preacher to pray for me and he asked
me to pray for myself. So that night when I went home from
the little church I went out into the horses' stall and knelt
down and asked God to save me. Then I prepared for bed and
knelt by the bed as I usually did for a good-night prayer and
asked God to forgive my sins and save me. I felt no change.
I did not have any glorious experience. I did not see any
light shining around about me. I did not hear the flutter of
angel wings. No electricity came in at my head or went out
at my fingers and toes! So I sadly went to bed without any
assurance of salvation. Then I thought, "Well, I had better
settle this thing for good someway or other;" so I got out of
bed and prayed again. There on my knees I thought how
strange it was that when I realized I was a sinner and that
there was nothing I could do to earn salvation and when God
had promised so plainly that He would save people and that
Jesus had died to pay for our sins—how strange, I thought,
that God would not save me! I decided I would leave the
matter in the hands of God the best I knew how and go to
bed.

I offered myself for membership in the church. I could not
feel any great conviction for sin, and yet I did not know that
I was saved. When, in that little west Texas church, they

asked me to stand and give my "experience," give my testimony before being received into the church, I simply said that I had thought about the matter a great deal, that I did not want to be a Methodist so I had decided to be a Baptist! I was a trembling, inexperienced boy, twelve years old. I was frightened at speaking before the people. And they someway had more confidence in my salvation than my testimony would have warranted, and received me in the church as a candidate for baptism!

When I was baptized I was strangely happy. Even yet I could give no clear testimony as to when I was saved or how. Oh, I wished that I knew just how and when I was saved and could know for sure that it was settled for good! But when others gave the very date and place when they were saved and told how happy they had been, I could not give any such experience.

Then one glad day I began reading the New Testament and came upon those wonderful promises in the Gospel of John, like clusters of ripe fruit on a beautiful tree!

"As many as received him, to them gave he power to become the sons of God, EVEN TO THEM THAT BELIEVE ON HIS NAME." John 1:12.

"He that believeth on the Son hath everlasting life."— John 3:36.

"Verily, verily, I say unto you, He that heareth my word, and believeth on him that sent me, hath everlasting life, and shall not come into condemnation; but is passed from death unto life."—John 5:24.

Oh, that last wonderful promise! I found that when I heard the Word of God and put my trust in the God who had sent His Son to save me, I then and there received everlasting life. I had often tried to remember that incident or that experience when I was nine years old and came to claim the Saviour publicly. I could not remember how I felt. I wondered if I had been as deeply moved as one must be to be saved. I recalled that a twelve-year-old boy who came the same day had been weeping and I had shed not a tear! I had thought many a time, "If I were really saved I would not do some of the things I do." But now I saw, praise the Lord, that when I had put my trust in Jesus Christ, then and there I received everlasting life! My doubts and fears were gone;

gone, thank God, forever! From that day to this I have never doubted for a moment that I am God's child. I know one thing beyond any doubt: when I trusted Jesus, depended on Him to forgive me, He did! The Word of God says so and that makes it so. On those promises I have hung the eternal welfare of my soul, and how sure, how unchanging is that blessed foundation for my faith!

4. How Foolish to Base One's Happiness and Assurance on Feelings!

Do you have doubts about your salvation? Do you sometimes wonder if you are truly a child of God? Then, dear friend, let me tell you something I have learned. It may comfort you to know that a great majority of the saints of God, before they became established in this sweet assurance based on the Word of God, have doubted and feared and trembled about their salvation. When they lived victoriously, then they felt sure of their salvation. When they fell into temptation or trouble, then they doubted whether they had ever been saved. Oh, feelings! Oh, emotions and experiences and ecstasies! What a foundation of shifting sand! How unreliable, how untrustworthy, how fleeting is all the assurance which one may have based upon one's feelings!

One man for long years had sweet confidence that he was saved, until he grew ill. His blood pressure was low and this brought about a natural depression and melancholy. Suddenly he began to have all kinds of doubts about his salvation. Satan, that old accuser of God's children, that enemy of a Christian's peace, takes advantage of every physical ailment, of every temptation to cause doubt and fear in the heart of a Christian who depends upon feelings.

A woman came to me who had been a happy Christian for many years. But when the change of life came on and her health was unstable, her mind became a victim of all kinds of fears, as is frequently the case at such a time. She had come now to believe that she must have committed the unpardonable sin! All her joys were gone. She still loved the Lord, still wanted to serve Him. She had no pleasure in the things of the world. But because now her physical condition led to a natural depression and because she was emotionally upset, as is very customary with many women at such a time, she feared that God had forsaken her. Oh, people who look within themselves and examine their feelings and emotions and try by these feelings and emotions to prove that they are born again, that they are children of God, will have many doubts and fears.

5. Knowing by the Dependable Record; Not by Feeling or Memory of a Feeling

But some preacher may boldly say that if you do not know for sure that you are saved, that if you do not have "an experience" that always satisfies you, then you are not saved. "If you can have it and not know it, then you could lose it without missing it," wisecracks some preacher. And he may say, "I know I was saved because I was there when it happened." Now that is really a very witty saying. It sounds so smart that one may not instantly recognize that such a man is depending not on the Word of God but upon his own changeable emotions and feelings and memories. Actually, the fact that you were there when it happened does not automatically guarantee that you will understand fully what happened and that you will always have perfect assurance of salvation.

Let me illustrate. "I was there when it happened," when I was born into the world the first time. Remember that salvation is simply a new birth. If one can know all about his second birth by the simple fact that he was there, then he ought to be able to know about his first birth for the same reason! Now I was born on December 11, 1895, in Cooke County, Texas. How do I know? Do you suppose that on that eventful day I sat up and looked about me and said, "Well! I see by the calendar that it is December 11, just two weeks before Christmas Eve! I'll put this down in my notebook so I will always remember I was born on December 11!" Do you suppose that I looked at my mother and said, "Your name, please, lady? I want to put it down in my notebook so I will always know who was my mother, who was my father, and the other conditions surrounding my birth." I did nothing of the kind! When I was born I did not know much of anything except when I got hungry. I learned gradually to know my mother's voice and to know when I was uncomfortable with dirty clothes or with the pricking of an unfastened safety pin. I later learned to focus both eyes and look at one object! Then I learned, I suppose, to smile when people tickled me under the chin. There were long months before I grew a single tooth, and other months before I learned to walk and talk. It is true that "I was there when it happened" at my first birth. But I was very young at the time, I took no note of my surroundings, and I cannot trust my memory about the matter at all!

And yet I know; in fact, it is beyond any doubt at all in my mind, that I was really born on December 11, 1895, that William H. Rice was my father, that Sallie LaPrade Rice was my mother, and that Gertrude was my sister, eighteen months older. How do I know? That is easy! I have it on the authority of my mother. It was written down in the family Bible. And recently I saw it written down on a separate piece of paper in my mother's own handwriting. There it was listed by her sweet fingers, "Gertrude Frances, born July 24, 1894. John R., born December 11, 1895 . . ." and so on with Ruth and George and baby Porter! I have the written record of one I absolutely trust. And so I know when I was born and who were my mother and my father.

And, thank God, I have even better assurance than that about my second birth! I have the written record of God's own Word saying that when I put my trust in Jesus Christ I passed from death to life! I have the written record that "he that believeth on the Son hath everlasting life" (John 3:36). I believed in Him, trusted Him, depended on Him to forgive me. Now I know He has done it because He never failed to keep His word, and He never will!

I know that Jesus said, "All that the Father giveth me shall come to me; and him that cometh to me I will in no wise cast out" (John 6:37). When I came to Christ it was because God the Father had given me to Jesus and put it in my heart to come! And then when I came He did not reject me, did not send me away, did not cast me out. He promised that He did not and would not. When I came to Jesus, He received me. I *know*, because I have the plain Word of God that cannot lie, that "him that cometh to me I will in no wise cast out."

When I say I came to Christ I do not mean when I joined the church or when I was baptized or when I walked down an aisle or when I took the preacher's hand. I mean that in my heart I wanted Christ, I wanted forgiveness, and I decided to trust Him and chose to come to Him. In my mind and heart, when I decided to come to Jesus, I had already come, then, in His sight. And when I came He received me, He forgave me. That is far better assurance than my feelings and my emotions.

"Whosoever shall call upon the name of the Lord shall be saved" (Rom. 10:13). I know that I called on the Lord. And I know God is not trying to trip me up, not trying to take advantage of my ignorance. I know that He sees the heart and He knows I wanted salvation, that I offered myself to Him and depended on Him to save me. An honest God knows that this poor sinner called on Him for salvation and turned the matter over to Him. Therefore, I have perfect assurance that I have the salvation which He promised. God cannot lie! And on His written record I claim that I have a contract with Him that He cannot and will not break. Oh, God *wants* to save sinners. He gave His Son to die on the cross to save sinners. And one who honestly, in his heart, calls on God for mercy and forgiveness and salvation, is assured of salvation by this clear promise of the Bible.

"Then they that gladly received his word were baptized," we are told of the new converts at Pentecost (Acts 2:41).

If the promise, "Whosoever shall call upon the name of the Lord shall be saved," seems too good to be true, too easy a plan of salvation, let us remember that the next verse, Romans 10:14, says, "How then shall they call on him in whom they have not believed?" Actually, one who calls upon Christ for mercy and forgiveness has trusted Christ in the heart, and the prayer of the heart is simply the manifestation of faith. How would one call on God for mercy and forgiveness if he did not believe there is a God who hears and that God has provided a way of salvation? You see, saving faith is in the heart of one who honestly, penitently calls upon Christ for salvation.

Have you the assurance of salvation based upon the plain Word of God? How precious is this assurance!

Here is another promise to hang the destiny of your soul upon with sweet assurance. Romans 10:8, 9 says: "But what saith it? The word is nigh thee, even in thy mouth, and in thy heart: that is, the word of faith, which we preach; That if thou shalt confess with thy mouth the Lord Jesus, and shalt believe in thine heart that God hath raised him from the dead, thou shalt be saved."

It is so near, so easy! Any penitent heart wanting to be forgiven, wanting to be made new, wanting to be cleansed, can turn and have it settled in a moment, because the word is near, this word of faith, that is, even in your mouth and your heart. What is it? Can you honestly confess with your mouth the Lord Jesus, believing in your heart that God raised Him up from the dead? Then that, this Scripture says, is saving faith!

There are two simple parts to this promise. Take the last part first. Do you believe that God raised Jesus from the dead? That proves His deity. Do you believe that Jesus really paid for our sins and rose for our justification, and that therefore He is God's own Lamb given to save us? Now if you believe that this resurrected Son is God come in the flesh (as His resurrection proves), are you ready to claim Him as your own Saviour? That is what God here requires. And He says simply that anybody who claims Christ, believing that He is God's own resurrected Son, is saved!

It is so simple as this: every one who is willing to take Christ, God's own resurrected Son, as his Saviour, can have Him. And one who thus believing in Christ claims Him is instantly saved!

The very minimum is required. If you know that God raised up Jesus from the dead, then you know that He is not an ordinary man. He is God's Son, our Saviour. Now if you trust in that kind of a Saviour enough to claim Him, that is enough to insure your salvation! So says the Word of God. And you who have so trusted Christ and claimed Him have an argument that you have a right to bring before God or anybody else that you are saved! According to the Word of God you can *know* that you have passed from death to life, on the authority of God.

6. Do You Make God a Liar, Doubting His Word?

Let us go back to the passage in I John, chapter 5. We noticed it above, and found that it plainly promised that one may know that he has eternal life. But now consider the whole passage, I John 5:9-13:

"If we receive the witness of men, the witness of God is greater: for this is the witness of God which he hath testified of his Son. He that believeth on the Son of God hath the witness in himself: he that believeth not God hath made him a liar; because he believeth not the record that God gave of his Son. And this is the record, that God hath given to us eternal life, and this life is in his Son. He that hath the Son hath life; and he that hath not the Son of God hath not life. These things have I written unto you that believe on the name of the Son of God; that ye may know that ye have eternal life, and that ye may believe on the name of the Son of God."

How strange that anyone would receive the witness of men instead of the witness of God! Now God has given a certain witness concerning His Son. "He that believeth on the Son of God hath the witness in himself." That is, Christ Himself comes into the heart and saves the soul through the regenerating work of the Holy Spirit. Thus one has within himself the new nature and the indwelling Spirit of God, as witness that he is saved. And one who does not believe what God has written on this matter makes God a liar "because he believeth not the record that God gave of his Son."

And then God gives us plainly again the written record, which we are to believe; and thus to know that we are saved.

"And this is the record, that God hath given to us eternal life, and this life is in his Son. He that hath the Son hath life; and he that hath not the Son of God hath not life."

Then comes this blessed promise: "These things have I written unto you that believe on the name of the Son of God; that ye may know that ye have eternal life, and that ye may believe on the name of the Son of God."

Will you believe this record, put down in the Bible so you might know for sure that you are saved? Are you ready to believe God on the matter and risk Christ on this naked word of Scripture? If you have trusted Christ, He says you are saved. If you have opened the door and received Christ, then you have everlasting life. Oh, today put your trust in Jesus and then know by the Scriptures that you have eternal life!

If one reads this who has not trusted in Christ alone for salvation, I beg you in Jesus' name to trust Him today and take the salvation so freely offered.

Now, dear doubting friend who may read this, will you throw away your doubts and risk the plain Word of God? Or will you make God a liar by doubting His Word?

Now one who bases his assurance on the plain Word of God may have other assurances also. He may love other Christians in a way that a lost man cannot love them. And thus he may know that he is saved, according to I John 3:14 which says, "We know that we have passed from death unto life, because we love the brethren. He that loveth not his brother abideth in death." The Christian graces will develop in a good Christian so that he can have an added assurance of his salvation in the fact that he has a love for Christians in his heart. But I remind you that this is not the main assurance. The main assurance is the record God has written which, He said, is written "unto you that believe on the name of the Son of God; that ye may know that ye have eternal life . . ." But there is a sweet added assurance when we discover that we love Christian people as an unsaved person cannot love Christians.

Again, a Christian will find as he grows in grace that he keeps God's commandments. Not perfectly, of course. All of us are sinful and weak. "If we say that we have no sin, we deceive ourselves, and the truth is not in us," says I John 1:8. Yet a Christian does love the Word of God and does want to please God. There is something in every born-again Christian that hates sin and wants to keep God's commandments. If a Christian lives near the Lord and grows in grace, he will find that sweet added assurance of his salvation. "And hereby we do know that we know him, if we keep his commandments" (I John 2:3).

Should a Christian have joy? Yes, and thank God I have much of it. How many, many times the Lord has been so near to me! Sometimes I have rejoiced in His presence so that I have laughed aloud for joy. Sometimes I have said over and over again, "Praise the Lord! Praise the Lord!" It is very sweet and precious to be conscious of the Lord's presence and to know that He hears our prayers and answers them and to know that He has His power upon us and will use us. I have such feelings and such joys, praise His name! But when feelings fade or change or disappear, thank God,

I have the solid rock of God's Word that never changes! God still loves the world! It is still true that God gave His Son, Jesus, to die for sinners! It is still true that the Scripture says, "Whosoever believeth in him should not perish, but have everlasting life." Bless God, when I change, the Bible does not change! When my feelings change, my emotions, God's blessed truth does not change. And I know that I am God's child, that He still has not cast me out, because He said He would not. I know that I have everlasting life and shall not come into condemnation, but am passed from death unto life, because Jesus in John 5:24 plainly says so. Oh, praise the Lord for the solid assurance of the Word of God that one who comes to Jesus Christ and trusts Him for forgiveness is saved! Salvation is by faith in Christ, not faith in one's emotions. So the strongest assurance is by the Word.

I urge everyone who reads this, then, to throw away all your doubts and depend from this time forth on what God has promised in the Word and what Jesus has done on the cross and is doing now as our High Priest at the right hand of God. Our sins are paid for! And if we have trusted Him for salvation we are saved. We know so because He said so! How blessed are those who know they are saved and who have this assurance based on the Word of God.

So we are told about the converts at Pentecost that "they that gladly received his word were baptized."

CHAPTER II

BAPTISM
Second Secret of a Happy, Prosperous Christian Life

IN THE GREAT revival at Pentecost the converts were baptized. "They that gladly received his word were baptized: and the same day there were added unto them about three thousand souls." Those who want to be happy, successful and prosperous, like the converts were at Pentecost, should follow the same plan. Those who know they have trusted Christ for salvation should then be baptized to show their faith in Christ.

1. How Important Jesus Made Baptism!

It is rather surprising how much importance is given to baptism in the New Testament. Jesus Himself was baptized in the River Jordan before the multitude, by John the Baptist (Luke 3:21, 22). There the Holy Spirit came visibly upon Him in form like a dove. John the Baptist had baptized multitudes of repentant, believing people. Now Jesus, through His disciples, baptized more than John (John 4:1, 2).

In the Great Commission Jesus gave strict orders about baptism. As it is given in Matthew 28:19, 20, Jesus said: "Go ye therefore, and teach all nations, baptizing them in the name of the Father, and of the Son, and of the Holy Ghost: Teaching them to observe all things whatsoever I have commanded you: and, lo, I am with you alway, even unto the end of the world." All the new converts were to be baptized on profession of their faith in Christ.

In Mark 16:15, 16 the command is given again: "Go ye into all the world, and preach the gospel to every creature. He that believeth and is baptized shall be saved; but he that believeth not shall be damned." Note that baptism was such a natural and customary accompaniment to a profession of faith in Christ that "he that believeth and is baptized" is the form in which Jesus said it. And you will see that Jesus did not mean that baptism was essential to salvation, because the same verse plainly says, "But he that believeth not shall be damned." Not to trust Jesus Christ personally is the cause of damnation. But those who trust Christ and are saved would naturally then follow His command to be baptized. In John 3:36 we are plainly told, "He that believeth on the Son hath everlasting life." This one who believed in Christ was saved before he was baptized, but was expected to be baptized, and of course when he was baptized he was still saved. But one who did not trust in Christ would be damned. Salvation was settled by personal faith in Christ, but it was naturally taken for granted that those who trusted Christ would be baptized.

And that is the way it happened in the New Testament, just as Jesus intimated that it should be. At Pentecost the believers were baptized at once. The Ethiopian eunuch, when Philip taught him the way of salvation, understood that after trusting Christ he should be baptized. And he was baptized there in a wayside stream or pond (Acts 8:38). Lydia and her household, when they trusted in Christ, were baptized (Acts 16:15). The jailer and his household were baptized the same hour of the night after they had heard the gospel and after they had obeyed the plain command and promise, "Believe on the Lord Jesus Christ, and thou shalt be saved, and thy house" (Acts 16:31-33).

In Acts 2:38, 39 we are taught that the attitude of mind that is properly exhibited in baptism is required for the fullness of the Holy Spirit. It is not that the outward rite of baptism will guarantee that one is filled with the Holy Spirit, but that one who honestly gives himself up to God in the meaning which baptism normally teaches is therefore prepared for the fullness of the Spirit for God's work.

Thus any Christian who cares about the words of Jesus and the practice of the New Testament Christians must seriously face the duty of being baptized. Baptism never saves a sinner. Salvation takes more than water, whether a spoonful or a tankful. Yet one who has been saved ought to be baptized because Jesus plainly commanded it, and because it is a public declaration of his faith in Christ, a public confession. And the meaning of baptism is so rich that many a Christian misses the fullest blessing and fullest prosperity by disobeying Christ in this matter.

2. The Meaning of Baptism

I do not mean here to go into the form of baptism. I have done that elsewhere in my book, *Bible Baptism*. I should rather leave that aside for the moment. The meaning and spirit of baptism are far more important than the form. I do not want to bring in any unnecessary controversy. I want this message to be a help to every new convert who will read it, of every denomination. By the study of the Word of God and the counsel and help of Bible-believing pastors the reader will be enabled to study further the matter of the mode of baptism. So we will not discuss it here. We are concerned here about the spiritual meaning which God intended baptism to have and why baptism is a step in happiness and prosperity and spiritual success for every Christian.

That meaning of baptism is made clear, I think, in Romans 6:1-8 as follows:

"What shall we say then? Shall we continue in sin, that grace may abound? God forbid. How shall we that are dead to sin, live any longer therein? Know ye not, that so many of us as were baptized into Jesus Christ were baptized into his death? Therefore we are buried with him by baptism into death: that like as Christ was raised up from the dead by the glory of the Father, even so we also should walk in newness of life. For if we have been planted together in the likeness of his death, we shall be also in the likeness of his resurrection: Knowing this, that our old man is crucified with him, that the body of sin might be destroyed, that henceforth we should not serve sin. For he that is dead is freed from sin. Now if we be dead with Christ, we believe that we shall also live with him."

Everyone who was baptized was baptized with reference to Christ and with reference to His death. Baptism pictured the burial and resurrection of Christ, so we are told that everyone who was baptized in Bible times thus pointed to the death and burial and resurrection of Jesus Christ. Christ died for us; so the new convert is counted dead to sin, dead to the old life. And when the new convert is baptized and comes out of the water in the likeness of Christ's resurrection, he means that now he counts himself dead to the old life and not to be controlled by it any more. He is dead in Christ and risen with Christ. His sins have been paid for by the Saviour's death, and he is free. But now he is raised up to live a new life for God. He is not to count himself the same man at all. He is no longer supposed to be under the dominion of sin and death. Although he is yet in a natural body, subject to some of the weakness and the coming death that sin brings, yet the Christian is to reckon himself a new creature, and so to live out-and-out for God.

Every new convert, then, when he is baptized, says to himself, to the world and to God, "I'm not my own any more! The old sinner that I was is now dead. Now I am a new creature. I will live a new life. I am raised up to live for Jesus Christ alone."

I maintain that every person who was ever baptized and did not mean to count the old sinful self dead and to overrule it and override it and keep it down, and thus to live a life surrendered to God and pleasing to God in the power of the Holy Spirit, falsified his testimony when he was baptized. It was a lie, a wicked lie, a hypocritical profession, if one was baptized and did not mean to lay self on the altar, unreservedly, to live for Jesus Christ.

When Jesus was baptized He had in mind His own coming crucifixion, His burial and resurrection. He did not shrink from it but gave Himself openly to the plan of the Father for Himself. And Jesus said, "Thus it becometh us to fulfill all righteousness" (Matt. 3:15). If it were suitable for Jesus to be baptized, picturing His own coming death, burial and resurrection, then it is suitable for a Christian to follow the example of His Saviour and to be baptized picturing the same thing—the Saviour's death for us, our death to sin in His death, and our glorious future resurrection pictured in His resurrection.

Can you see, then, how important it is for a Christian to be baptized? To be baptized means to put on the uniform of your king, to take the oath of allegiance, to publicly claim your Saviour. To be baptized means a conscious giving up one's own way and a full surrender to the will of God. To be baptized means giving self up to crucifixion, to live a resurrected life for God. Every Christian ought to have that time of surrender, that time of holy dedication, that time of reckoning himself dead. In fact, it ought to be the first great decision that every Christian makes after he has taken Christ as his Saviour. And that decision ought to be confirmed by the outward rite of baptism.

The world, it is true, often does not understand the meaning of baptism. And yet this much at least is true—everyone who sees a new convert baptized understands that the new convert means now to live for Christ.

I remember the joy that welled up in my heart on that cold November day when, at a little artificial lake or "tank" in west Texas, I followed my Saviour in baptism. How my heart warmed! I did not know all the doctrine involved, and I was not even as thoroughly sure of my salvation as I afterward became. But, thank God, I felt in my heart the approval of the Saviour because I had publicly taken my stand for Him and had publicly announced my intention to serve Him at any cost for the rest of my days. How many, many times I have seen joy unspeakable fill the faces of new converts as they followed the Saviour in baptism!

So, young Christian, if you would be happy, make that great decision and consecration that is properly involved in baptism and obey the Saviour in this blessed pictorial ceremony. Use for Christ this object lesson that pictures the death of Christ and His resurrection and our faith in this crucified, risen Saviour, and our surrender with all our souls to serve Him and live His life.

A great southern preacher has called our attention to the fact that Jesus left two object lessons, "the gospel for the eye," that ought to keep straight forever the great doctrine of salvation by the atoning blood of Christ. When one makes profession of his faith in Christ and is publicly baptized, it pictures that Jesus died and rose again, died for our sins and rose for our justification. And every time one takes the Lord's Supper he reminds himself and others that only by the death of Christ, only by His body broken on the tree and His blood poured out on the cross are we saved and made fit for Heaven.

How important it is then, that everybody should be reminded that we believe in the death of Christ, that we count ourselves crucified with Him and raised to live for Him. And this holy resolution of the heart is publicly announced in baptism. Every new convert, then, should follow the example of those at Pentecost. "They that gladly received his word were baptized" (Acts 2:41). Thus one will be obeying also the plain command of Jesus Christ in the Great Commission.

▧▨▧▨▧▨▧▨▧▨▧▨▧▨ CHAPTER III

CHURCH MEMBERSHIP
Third Secret of Christian Happiness and Blessing

SO MANY CHURCHES (we here mean local congregations) have failed God, have turned away from loyalty to the Word of God and Christ's soul-winning program as given in the Great Commission, that it has become customary among many Bible-believing people to make light of local church membership. Now I would not encourage anybody to join with unbelievers in Christ and the Bible, in churches or anywhere else. I would not encourage any Christian ever to give a dime to a modernist who denies the deity of Christ, the inspiration of the Bible and Christ's atoning death on the cross. I am not saying that it is all right to join any church, whether it is true to Christ or not. But I do say as plainly as I know how that every Christian ought to join in with some local congregation of born-again Christians. He ought to do this for his own good and for the good of other Christians, and to help carry on the work of Jesus Christ.

1.   Local Churches in New Testament Times

Were there churches, local congregations of Christians, banded together in New Testament times? There certainly were such churches. Of about 110 times that the word *church* or *churches* appears in our English Bible, at least ninety of these times the word refers to a local congregation of Christians or to more than one local congregation of Christians. The Bible speaks continually of "the church of God at Corinth" or "the church at Rome" or "the church that is in thy house" or "the churches of Galatia" or "the seven churches of Asia." The regular language of the New Testament refers continually to local congregations of Christians, as separate, complete churches.

These churches had simple but definite organization. They had deacons (Acts 6:1-6) to help wait on the poor of the congregation. In Jerusalem these deacons were appointed by the apostles and ordained, after they had been selected by the people (Acts 6:3). Elders, or pastors, were appointed or elected in the churches, also. Paul admonished the church in Corinth to come together and officially withdraw fellowship from a certain man living in sin, "to deliver such an one unto Satan for the destruction of the flesh, that the spirit may be saved in the day of the Lord Jesus." They were to do this "in the name of our Lord Jesus Christ, when ye are gathered together . . ." (I Cor. 5:4, 5). Saul (later called Paul the apostle), was converted, and returned to Jerusalem where "he assayed to join himself to the disciples: but they were all afraid of him, and believed not that he was a disciple" (Acts 9:26). But good Barnabas took Saul's part, convinced the apostles that Saul had been converted, and thereafter he was received among the people as a Christian. We would say that Paul "joined the church," that is, that he joined the assembly of Christians at Jerusalem and became known as one of them. But he was rejected until it was proved that he had truly been converted.

After that wonderful revival at Pentecost, the new converts joined in the assembly, the church at Jerusalem. "Then they that gladly received his word were baptized: AND THE SAME DAY THERE WERE ADDED UNTO THEM ABOUT THREE THOUSAND SOULS" (Acts 2:41). It is clear that these three thousand were carefully questioned, were baptized and enrolled in the local assembly. Thereafter "they continued stedfastly in the apostles' doctrine [teaching] and fellowship, and in breaking of bread . . ." (vs. 42). Continually, "The Lord added to the church daily such as should be saved" (vs. 47). And throughout the account of the New Testament Christians at Jerusalem much is made of their sweet fellowship, their sacrificial serving of one another, their hospitality one to another, eating from house to house.

2. The Benefits of Church Membership

There are many, many reasons why every new convert should join in with other Christians in a local church and there serve God.

First, a Christian needs Christian fellowship and Christian company. Nobody in the world can live a good Christian life without keeping good company. Bad company ruined Samson, the Spirit-filled judge of Israel, and led him to commit terrible sins so that the Spirit of the Lord departed from him. Bad company ruined Solomon. In his old age he married heathen wives and they led him into idolatry. Bad company caused Simon Peter to lose his courage, to deny the Lord and to curse and swear! Oh, young Christian, you cannot possibly live at your best as a Christian unless you seek the company of other Christians.

Someone says, "I can live as well outside the church as in the church." No you cannot! How could anyone live as well running with the Devil's crowd as he could running with the

Lord's crowd? How could anyone live as well with the bad influence of the Christ-rejectors and the God-haters as he could live with the prayers and counsel and encouragement of Christians? It is better for a Christian to work with other Christians in a job. He is more likely to find a good job with Christians in the church than out of it. It is right for a Christian to marry only a Christian. He is more likely to marry a Christian if he attends the church with other Christians.

Second, one needs the public services of the church. He needs to sing, and people sing better in groups. He needs to hear Christian testimony. He needs to join others in earnest prayer and have others pray with him and for him.

Third, the Christian needs a pastor. One needs to hear preaching, but one needs also to be under the spiritual supervision of some pastor who holds himself accountable to God for his soul. One needs to have a pastor as a spiritual father, or as a spiritual overseer. In fact, the word *pastor* means overseer or superintendent, and Christians need their Christian lives superintended by godly, Spirit-filled men. God knew what He was doing when He gave orders for local New Testament congregations, called churches, and planned for them to have pastors and teachers and to meet in public assembly.

Fourth, a Christian ought to have some place where he can go regularly to be taught the Word of God. Whether it is in Sunday School or in the preaching service, the church owes a duty to its members and every member ought to take advantage of the privilege that is afforded to learn the Word of God.

Fifth, every Christian ought to have some place where it would be convenient to do much of his Christian giving. Every Christian ought to support the preaching of the gospel by supporting his pastor. Every Christian ought to support mission work, and usually that is most easily done and most properly done through a church. Every Christian ought to have some part in the relief of the Christian poor, and often that is done better through the church than by individual charity, or by the lodges, or by government relief agencies. Christians ought to do the work of Christians, and most of these things they do better in churches than they can do outside of churches.

I have found that many love the Lord who do not join churches. But they are irresponsible Christians. They do not have anybody in authority over them whose word they eminently respect and follow. They do not hold themselves to some strict schedule of serving God, or of worship, or of giving. They feel no responsibility for getting the gospel out to others about them. It is important that every Christian should get in with other Christians, have fellowship with other Christians, feel a responsibility to a local church and be ministered to by a local church.

Therefore, I urge every convert, for your own happiness and for the good of the cause of Christ, to find a church that believes the Bible; a church where the gospel is preached and souls are saved; and help to make that church stronger by your membership and by your prayers and your example and testimony and gifts. So they did in the revival at Pentecost.

CHAPTER IV

THE BIBLE

Fourth Secret of Christian Happiness and Prosperity

WE ARE TOLD about the new converts at Pentecost that ". . . they continued stedfastly in the apostles' doctrine . . ." (Acts 2:42). Well, we have no apostles alive now, and yet the apostles' doctrine is with us. The Apostle John wrote some of it in the Gospel of John, in the First, Second, and Third Epistles of John, and in the book of Revelation. Matthew wrote part of it in the Gospel According to Matthew. Peter wrote part of it in the First and Second Epistles of Peter. Paul the apostle wrote some of it in the thirteen books of the New Testament (fourteen if we count Hebrews from Paul, as I think we should). The Bible we now have is the same apostles' doctrine that New Testament Christians followed. The apostles and other preachers preached the Old Testament and they had divinely revealed to them the doctrine, the teaching which is now in our New Testament, and they passed this on to the people. So if we set out to continue stedfastly in the Word of God we will be doing the same thing as these converts of the revival at Pentecost did.

1. Wonderful Promises to Those Who Read, Memorize, Meditate Upon and Follow the Word of God

I think we may safely say that the Christian's use of the Bible is the most important factor of all in securing Christian happiness and success and every blessing of God upon His child. You see, if a Christian knows the Bible, loves the Bible, follows the Bible, and spiritually understands the Bible, he will already have all the other of the seven secrets we are naming in this book. The Christian who has the Bible has the road map for the Christian pilgrim, the orders for the Christian soldier. The Bible maps out the way to find all the hidden treasures a Christian needs, all that is necessary to make him happy, useful and successful.

With this in mind we should not be surprised to find many wonderful promises about what the Bible will do for the Christian.

The *reading* of the Bible is blessed of God. And if one cannot read, it is equally blessed to hear, just so the Christian keeps the things that are written in the Book. For Revelation 1:3 says, "Blessed is he that readeth, and they that hear the words of this prophecy, and keep those things which are written therein: for the time is at hand." *Knowing* and *loving* the Bible will help a Christian to have his prayers answered. For John 15:7 says, "If ye abide in me, and my words abide in you, ye shall ask what ye will, and it shall be done unto you." Christ says that the Christian who is wrapped up in Christ, absorbed in Christ, wholly surrendered to and occupied with Christ, and provided His Word abides in the Christian, may ask anything he wishes! One thoroughly committed to Christ can be trusted in his will, when he knows enough of the Bible to know the will of God and to know what will please and honor God. A proper understanding of and devotion to the Bible is so closely connected with having our prayers answered!

The blessed Word of God, as we read it regularly and absorb it and love it, will help us conquer the sins in our own lives. "Wherewithall shall a young man cleanse his way? by taking heed thereto according to thy word," says Psalm 119:9. This means that it is an impossibility for a Christian to live an overcoming life without taking heed to his life according to the Word of God. That is the reason David said, by divine inspiration, "Thy word have I hid in mine heart, that I might not sin against thee" (Psa. 119:11).

A knowledge of the Word of God will guide us in the way we should go, guide us in our decisions of right and wrong, and in our choices. For Psalm 119:24 says, "Thy testimonies also are my delight and my counsellors." In that same great chapter on the Word of God, Psalm 119:105 says, "Thy word is a lamp unto my feet, and a light unto my path." Since we know that the Bible is the very Word of God, doesn't it seem silly that any Christian should presume to know how to live and have wisdom to meet life's daily problems without being familiar with this rich and miraculous letter from God, the Bible?

Now let me give one of the strongest promises in the whole Bible. How wonderfully reassuring is this promise to the young Christian! It is given in Psalm 1:1-3.

"Blessed is the man that walketh not in the counsel of the ungodly, nor standeth in the way of sinners, nor sitteth in the seat of the scornful. But his delight is in the law of the Lord; and in his law doth he meditate day and night. And he shall be like a tree planted by the rivers of water, that bringeth forth his fruit in his season; his leaf also shall not wither; and whatsoever he doeth shall prosper."

The blessed or fortunate or happy man described in this psalm is one that does not walk in the counsel of the ungodly, does not stand in the way of sinners and never sits in the seat of the scornful. The young Christian should be careful, of course, to keep good company, to walk with Christian people and never to be influenced by bad companions.

But the positive condition here mentioned which is to bring immeasurable blessing is that the blessed man has his delight in the Bible and meditates in it day and night. "His delight is in the law of the Lord; and in his law doth he meditate day and night."

Now what shall be the daily and continuing results? This Christian, meditating day and night in the Bible, ". . . shall be like a tree planted by the rivers of water, that bringeth forth his fruit in his season; his leaf also shall not wither; and whatsoever he doeth shall prosper." In west Texas where there is not much moisture one does not find great forests of trees extending over the countryside. There may be small brushy mesquite and other shrubs, but when one sees tall cottonwoods and other large trees growing in a thin line in some valley, he may know that that marks a creek, a water course. There great trees may rise tall and strong because their roots are down in the moist earth about a stream of water or a watercourse where at least in rainy times the water runs. So is the Bible-believing, Bible-reading and Bible-meditating Christian in this spiritually drought-stricken world! The leaf of his Christian joy and testimony never withers! He always brings forth fruit in his season. And everything he puts his hand to prospers! What a wonderful promise for a Christian!

And what is the river of water into which the Christian tree may push his roots and so always be sure of green leaves and of heavy fruitage? It is the Bible, the Word of God! And how does a Christian draw from this inexhaustible source of help and strength and happiness and fruit? He meditates on the Word of God day and night; he delights in the Word of God, absorbs it and lives by it!

A similar promise was given to Joshua when he succeeded Moses as commander of the Israelites and led them into the land of Canaan. The Lord promised to be with Joshua as He had been with Moses, never to forsake him nor fail him. Here are the words of encouragement and of command and promise given to Joshua:

"Only be thou strong and very courageous, that thou mayest observe to do according to all the law, which Moses my servant commanded thee: turn not from it to the right hand or to the left, that thou mayest prosper whithersoever thou goest. This book of the law shall not depart out of thy mouth; but thou shalt meditate therein day and night, that thou mayest observe to do according to all that is written therein: for then thou shalt make thy way prosperous, and then thou shalt have good success."—Josh. 1:7, 8.

Joshua was to be very careful to observe all of the law (the part of the Bible they then had). He was to turn not from it to the right or to the left in order "that thou mayest prosper whithersoever thou goest." The Book of the Law was not to depart out of Joshua's mouth. He was to read it, think of it, talk about it all the time, day and night. "But thou shalt meditate therein day and night, that thou mayest observe to do according to all that is written therein." And then comes the wonderful promise, just like that in Psalm 1:3, "For then thou shalt make thy way prosperous, and then thou shalt have good success."

You see, then, that a Christian does have a definite promise that if he fulfills certain conditions he shall have good success, he shall make his way prosperous. Or in the words of Psalm 1:3, the man who meditates day and night in the Word of God to follow it—"whatsoever he doeth shall prosper." Let me insist, then, that the young Christian start out from the very first to love the Bible, read the Bible, meditate over it, study it, and learn it and live by it! This is the greatest single secret of success that I can give, for it will lead the honest heart aright about all the other duties and privileges of a Christian.

2. Suggestions to the Young Christian About the Use of the Bible

I once helped a young man to find peace and joy again after he had backslidden and lost his joy and assurance. Then I said to him, "You must set out now to read the Word of God and use it."

He answered hastily: "But I do! I read a verse of the Bible almost every day!" A *verse* of the Bible! Do you think that young fellow really strained himself in reading the Bible, a whole verse of it nearly every day? That kind of reading of the Bible will not do. That is childishly inadequate. It is foolish to suppose that anyone who treats the Bible like that, reading only a verse a day, can have its full strength and blessing.

Let me make some simple suggestions that will, if followed, certainly lead to happiness, prosperity and success for every Christian.

First of all, set out to read the Bible. I mean read all of it. I mean read it like you read other books, to enjoy it, to learn it, to absorb it, to be educated by it. I do not mean just a careless and piecemeal reading, but a thorough reading of the Bible. I suggest that every Christian set out to read the Bible through at least within a year. And that is a very simple and easy thing to do if you mean business. It will only require thatyou read one chapter a day in the NewTestament or the Psalms, and three chapters every day from the Old Testament, and you will read the entire Bible through in a little less than eleven months. It will require only a few minutes a day, it will help to develop a lifelong habit of orderliness and self-discipline. But best of all, it will acknowledge that God's Word is for you to know and it will certainly make it so God can help you to learn the Bible. You may have two book marks in your Bible, or three, and keep one in the Old Testament and one in the New (perhaps a third in the Psalms). Then every day read one full chapter in the New Testament or the Psalms and three chapters in the rest of the Old Testament besides the Psalms. Any Christian who has not read the whole Bible through, including all the genealogies, all the historical narratives, every line of it, ought to be ashamed of himself. He has never taken the Bible seriously. It is all God's Word and it ought to be read through, every line of it, frequently.

Let me urge, too, that one read through chapter after chapter in consecutive order, in any given book. The Psalms were divided up into separate chapters originally. They are not connected. It is about the same with the book of Proverbs. But in the rest of the Bible each book is a consecutive whole, and each ought to be read chapter after chapter through the whole book. When you start on Genesis, then keep going right on through Genesis until you finish it.

And let me suggest, too, that many times a whole book of the Bible ought to be read at one sitting. You might read the whole book of Genesis in one long evening or a Sunday afternoon and be wonderfully blessed by it, or likewise the books of Matthew or Luke or Acts. There are many shorter books of the Bible that can be read in fifteen or twenty minutes. You will gain much to take frequently a whole book at a time and read it through earnestly and carefully.

Then a Christian should set out to memorize a lot of the Bible. Mark the verses that are specially sweet and good which you plan to memorize. Some Christians try to do a little memory work every day, either to memorize one verse that is in the daily reading they have selected, or to refresh one's mind on an entire Psalm, for example. You will remember that David said, "Thy word have I hid in mine heart, that I might not sin against thee." A verse in the Bible that one has only read may not come up to warn him and reprove him and keep him from sin, but a verse that one has memorized and hid in the heart will surely do so. So be sure to memorize a lot of Scripture. I suggest that Christians should get my little booklet, *"What Must I Do to Be Saved?"* and memorize a lot of the verses used there in order to use them in personal soul winning. The Gospel of John has many verses on the plan of salvation, like John 1:12; John 3:14-18; John 3:36; John 5:24; John 6:37; John 6:40; John 6:47. But throughout the Bible there are many verses that one ought to know by heart to use in dealing with others.

Then every Christian ought to memorize some of the Psalms—Psalm 1, Psalm 23, Psalm 34, Psalm 103, Psalm 126, and many others. As you read over the Psalms, pick out some favorite Psalm which is not too long, learn it, say it over frequently and enjoy it. It will help to mold your life and make you happy and keep you near to God.

In the New Testament one certainly ought to memorize a good many Scriptures. Perhaps you should memorize John, chapter 14; or John, chapter 3; or Romans, chapter 8; or Romans, chapter 12; or I Corinthians, chapter 13. God will help you. But hide the Word of God in your heart, some of it every day if possible. How sweet it will be in the years to come and how blessed when it keeps you from sin and encourages you in prayer and gives you faith to call on God for greater things!

Reading the Bible is not enough, and even memorizing much of the Bible is not enough. The Christian is commanded to "meditate therein day and night." Have the Bible often in your mind. Ask God to help you think about it and enjoy it and delight in it. For it is in meditating on the Word of God that the Holy Spirit does His blessed work of developing the Christian graces in your heart and in giving you faith and in showing you what is wrong with your life, or how to have your prayers answered. or which course you should pursue. So take time to think about the Bible and meditate upon its teachings, its promises and its blessings.

And I need not say that any honest dealing with the Word of God will mean that the Christian is to live by what he finds therein. To read the Bible and not follow it would be hypocrisy. The new converts after the revival at Pentecost "continued stedfastly in the apostles' doctrine." And so you should make a holy vow, "By God's grace I will do what God makes clear in the Word of God. I will follow the Word of God in my life, as the Holy Spirit helps me to understand it and gives me grace to follow it." How precious is the life that is built upon the solid Word of God! How sure and believing will be your prayers, how confident your joy as you set out to follow the Word of God everywhere it leads! Oh, just to know and do the sweet will of God as revealed in the Bible! That surely is the highest way of life for a child of God and is the sure road to happiness, prosperity and success. Then the leaf of your Christian joy will not wither, you will bring forth fruit in season, according to the clear promise of God's Word, and whatsoever you do will prosper! What a rule for success is given us in Psalm 1:3!

 CHAPTER V

PRAYER

Fifth Secret of Christian Happiness and Blessing

THE YOUNG CONVERTS and the older Christians alike, after Pentecost, "continued stedfastly in the apostles' doctrine and fellowship, and in breaking of bread, AND IN PRAYERS," we are told (Acts 2:42). These Christians had certain plans that they followed regularly. Their lives had a definite pattern. The Word of God was first with them. They kept on following the apostles' doctrine. They kept up Christian fellowship and love and unity. They regularly broke bread, remembering, in the Lord's Supper, the death of Christ and their salvation by His blood, through faith. And they continually maintained their prayer life.

1. The Importance of the Christian's Prayer Life

In the Bible God talks to the Christian. In prayer the Christian talks to God. And if one really obeys the Bible he will be drawn more and more to prayer about everything. Prayer is the great resource of the Christian.

The young convert had as well remember at the very start that all around him there are evils which he cannot control nor overcome alone. Satan, who has lost the battle about keeping the soul away from God and salvation, still sets out to tempt the Christian, to cause him doubts and fears and troubles and to ruin his happiness and ruin his influence. The Christian who is to overcome Satan and live a victorious, happy life must be, not far away from God at any time, but able to go to his heavenly Father for strength and wisdom.

The work that a Christian is supposed to do will require miracles. For example, to save a soul is beyond any human strength or wisdom. It takes a miracle of God to make a black heart white, to make a child of God out of a child of the Devil. It takes a miracle, the working of the Holy Spirit of God, to save a soul. And any Christian who wants to win souls must, in the nature of the case, be in touch with God so he can call for God's power and God's wisdom and receive them.

A Christian ought to learn to live by prayer every day. The Christian should depend not on his labor for his daily bread, but on God. Perhaps he will labor all the more because he is a Christian, and do better work; yet still the Christian's dependence should be upon his heavenly Father. He should be able to pray for daily bread and get daily bread. He should be able to pray through any problem of sickness, or problems of a job, or marriage, or friends, or Christian service, or temptation. You see, "Prayer is the Christian's vital breath," and no one can live a good Christian life without being constantly in touch with God and on praying ground.

I am not surprised, therefore, that the new converts at Pentecost continued stedfastly in prayer, as we are told in the Bible that they did. And everywhere you find Christians who continue stedfastly in prayer, along with prayerful meditation and the following of the Word of God, you will have wonderfully victorious and happy Christians.

It is clear, then, that every Christian ought to pray every day. In fact, in the Lord's Prayer, given as our example, the Lord Jesus told us to pray, "Give us this day our daily bread." So we know that one should pray somewhat after that fashion every day.

2. Regular Times for Prayer

And prayer is so important that it should have some regular time, a time that would have priority, a time that would be remembered and honored daily. We think that eating is important enough to set apart regular times each day for eating. Sleeping is regarded as important enough that we set aside certain hours for sleeping. A job is counted important enough that a man is supposed to reserve certain hours, arriving on time and working through the full shift of his day. Then you may be sure, dear Christian, that you would be wise to religiously set aside certain times and seasons to pray and seek God's face every day.

Let me suggest also that the early morning is one of the very best times to pray. "Those that seek me early shall find me," the Lord has said in His Word (Prov. 8:17). Then we have the blessed example of our Saviour who prayed early in the morning. "And in the morning, rising up a great while before day, he went out, and departed into a solitary place, and there prayed" (Mark 1:35). Multitudes of Christians have found that to meet God early in the day and take time for prayer would make the whole day sweeter and would prevent many a heartache and many a careless sin.

3. Praying Without Ceasing

It is true that to have regular times of prayer is good. I hope the new convert will have a "morning watch" with the Lord regularly, before breakfast, if possible, or immediately after breakfast. But that is not enough praying for a Christian. For the Bible has many clear commands, teaching that one should pray continually and that prayer should get to be second nature to the Christian. One should become so conscious of the Lord's presence that he will be crying out to God about certain burdensome matters or about the salvation of souls or be in sweet communion with God about the Lord's work or the Christians' needs, all the time. Notice these clear commands of Scripture:

"And he spake a parable unto them to this end, that men ought always to pray, and not to faint."—Luke 18:1.

". . . continuing instant in prayer."—Rom. 12:12.

"Continue in prayer, and watch in the same with thanksgiving."—Col. 4:2.

"Praying always with all prayer and supplication in the Spirit, and watching thereunto with all perseverance and supplication for all saints."—Eph. 6:18.

"Pray without ceasing."—I Thess. 5:17.

Here we have five clear statements that a Christian ought to pray all the time! So when a Christian comes to prayer and says, "Heavenly Father, we come into Thy presence this morning . . ." it may mean that the Christian is wrong in not having remained in the Lord's presence, consciously, all the time!

Nothing can be sweeter than to pray all the time. A Christian ought to get to be conscious of the dear Lord's presence so that everything that is done is done as in the presence of God, and thus one can pour out his burdened heart to God about anything, and may do it continuously.

Let me earnestly urge, then, upon the Christian who wants to be happy, who wants to be blessed, who wants to be prospered, that he pray all the time and make prayer the biggest thing in his life.

4. Some Suggestions About How to Pray

Let me suggest some very simple rules that may be helpful to those who want to learn to pray as they ought.

First, remember that you are coming to your loving heavenly Father. I would try to learn never to speak *about* God in the third Person while in prayer. Talk *to* God, not *about* God. You do not need to say, "We want God to be with us." You should be able to say, "Dear heavenly Father, please be with me!" As that truth becomes real to you, that God is now your Father and that you are now His child, that you are His heir, that God who has given His Son for you will give anything else that is good for you, then surely it will be easier and sweeter to pray. Oh, come boldly! You are speaking to your own dear Father in Heaven.

Second, every Christian should remember that Christ, the same dear Lord Jesus who died on the cross to save us, is now at the right hand of the Father in Heaven, and there He intercedes for us. He is our Advocate, our Mediator, our Intercessor. He stands as our High Priest before God so that we know He takes our part, and that ought to give us great comfort as we come to pray.

In Hebrews 4:14-16 the Lord urges us to be bold when we come to pray, since we know that the Lord Jesus is there to take our part and He understands our weaknesses and has made atonement for our sins. Listen to that blessed promise and make it yours, young Christian:

"Seeing then that we have a great high priest, that is passed into the heavens, Jesus the Son of God, let us hold fast our profession. For we have not an high priest which cannot be touched with the feeling of our infirmities; but was in all points tempted like as we are, yet without sin. Let us therefore come boldly unto the throne of grace, that we may obtain mercy, and find grace to help in time of need." —Heb. 4:14-16.

Remember that there is mercy, wonderful mercy for you, to cover all your sins! Remember that the Lord Jesus knows about your infirmities and can be touched in His dear heart with the feeling of your need, your trouble, and your weakness. Though He Himself never sinned, yet He was tempted as much as you are and like you are about anything.

"Let us therefore come boldly to the throne of grace," we are entreated. There you may find mercy and you may find grace to help in any time of need.

Third, remember that a Christian has a right to take every burden he has to the Lord. We have this blessed exhortation, "Casting all your care upon him; for he careth for you" (I Pet. 5:7). We have the blessed invitation, "Cast thy burden upon the Lord, and he shall sustain thee" (Psa. 55:22). Do not think any burden too heavy and do not think any problem too trivial to bring to God. He wants to bear your burden. He wants you to trust Him about all your problems. Come, dear Christian, to your heavenly Father and so have your burden lifted and be happy.

In Philippians 4:6 we are commanded, "Be careful for nothing; but in every thing by prayer and supplication with

thanksgiving let your requests be made known unto God."
"In every thing"! You have a right to make your request to
God about everything. Ask everything your heart desires;
for Mark 11:24 says, "Therefore I say unto you, What things
soever ye desire, when ye pray, believe that ye receive them,
and ye shall have them." Pray for whatever would delight
your heart, for He has said, "Delight thyself also in the
Lord; and he shall give thee the desires of thine heart" (Psa.
37:4).

If you learn to take everything to God in prayer and stay
there and pray through, then you will find that the blessed
promise is true, as Philippians 4:7 says, "And the peace of
God, which passeth all understanding, shall keep your hearts
and minds through Christ Jesus."

> What a Friend we have in Jesus,
> All our sins and griefs to bear!
> What a privilege to carry
> EVERYTHING to God in prayer!
>
> Oh what peace we often forfeit,
> Oh what needless pain we bear,
> All because we do not carry
> EVERYTHING to God in prayer!

Fourth, I would encourage you, dear Christian, to claim
God's promises when you pray. You should learn them, mark
them in your Bible, review them again and again—such
promises as Jeremiah 33:3, as John 14:13, 14, as Mark 11:
24, as Mark 9:23. Learn the blessed promise of James 4:2,
of Matthew 18:19 and Matthew 21:22. God has many, many
promises and He wants you to know them, believe them and
claim them. And when you go to pray you will be perfectly
safe to quote any of these promises to God. For when you
meet God's promise you can certainly expect Him to meet
His own part as He has said He would. Remember that
praying according to the will of God means praying according to the Scriptures. And how successful that praying is,
praying according to the Scriptures!

Fifth, be as definite as possible. Why not keep a little
record book of specially urgent prayers? Put down the date
when you made the request of God, and keep on praying;
then put down the date when the answer comes right beside

or under the request. Now and then you would do well to weigh the desires of your heart until you can write down on paper briefly a list of the things that you honestly come to God in petition for. That will help to make your prayers definite. Do not keep the same list every day but amend it and change it as your heart's desire grows or is molded by the leading of the Holy Spirit, or as some answers come and other burdens arise which need prayer.

Sixth, let me urge upon you to pray through about your burdens. That means that you are not to quit easily, not to be discouraged, but to keep on praying. That is in the very nature of faith itself, and it is very precious to God. Read what Jesus said about how a poor widow prevailed with an unjust judge (Luke 18:1-8). Read the story of the Syrophenician woman, and how by her persistence she won the answer to her prayer and greatly pleased the dear Lord Jesus (Matt. 15:21-28). Read the story of the importunate friend who came knocking at a neighbor's house for bread and by his importunity won it (Luke 11:5-10). That shows how Christians should beg God and plead with God and wait on God to receive bread for sinners, soul-winning power. So do not give up easily, but keep on praying. If God shows you that your prayer is wrong, then ask Him to help you change it. But as long as you do not have clear evidence from the Word of God or by the Holy Spirit's leading that your prayer is wrong, then keep on praying. Ask God to change your desires if your prayer is wrong, or to give you faith to expect the blessing you seek if your prayer is right. Keep on praying!

Seventh, when you come to pray, be sure to confess your sins. Any honest child of God who stays near the Lord will find his heart grows very sensitive and tender about his sins. Oh, these hateful sins that creep into our lives! They grieve God; they will grieve us, too, if we stay very near Him and His Word. So take time to confess your shortcomings, your failures; take time to confess everything you know grieves God in your life. Do that every day. You will find that as you confess your sins, God forgives them and takes them out of the way and you will have a sweet assurance that He does not hold them against you. And more than that, by confessing your sin, you will find that God will give you more power to overcome sin and to live victoriously.

And, last, let me urge that when you come to pray you must be sure that you forgive others. For Jesus said we are to pray like this: "And forgive us our sins; for we also forgive every one that is indebted to us" (Luke 11:4). Jesus also plainly said, "For if ye forgive men their trespasses, your heavenly Father will also forgive you: but if ye forgive not men their trespasses, neither will your Father forgive your trespasses." Any Christian who does not forgive others finds that day by day differences pile up between him and God. He will find his fellowship with God broken. He will find the sweet Spirit of God is grieved and does not seem to lead as clearly as before. So if a Christian wants the daily cleansing, the daily renewal of fellowship, the daily taking of sin out of the way between him and God, he must forgive others when he comes to pray.

How merciful God has been to forgive us our sins and save us! And if we will but forgive others, how merciful He will be daily to cleanse us anew of our daily sins, though we are already saved. Those who would not grieve the Holy Spirit of God must put away bitterness and wrath and anger and clamor and evil-speaking and all malice, and remember, "Be ye kind one to another, tenderhearted, forgiving one another, even as God for Christ's sake hath forgiven you" (Eph. 4:30-32).

Prayer is one of the greatest steps to a happy, prosperous, successful Christian life. Dear Christian, take time, take time, take time to keep up your prayer life and keep things settled up with God all the time. Confess to Him all your sins, take to Him all your burdens, thank Him for all your blessings!

CHAPTER VI

GIVING
Sixth Secret, Putting God First With All Possessions

OF THE HAPPY Christians at Jerusalem after Pentecost we are told that ". . . all that believed were together, and had all things common; and sold their possessions and goods, and parted them to all men, as every man had need" (Acts 2: 44, 45).

What a remarkable effect it had on these Jewish people when they were converted to Christ, when they were assured of their salvation by the Word of God, when they were baptized, joined the local assembly, set out to follow stedfastly the apostles' doctrine, and continued in prayer! They were happy Christians, victorious Christians. And they seemed to have committed all their possessions to God and stopped worrying about whether they would have food and clothes and housing for the future. What a wonderful example of happy trust, of Christian fellowship and mutual care one for another!

And one of the important principles on which a new convert must live, if he is to be a really happy, prosperous and victorious Christian, is that he must put God first on the money question. He must learn that everything he is and everything he has belongs to God. He must set out to please God by the way he handles all his possessions, and symbolize this by the way he gives to the Lord's cause.

There are a number of lessons that a young Christian can learn from these Christians at Jerusalem who were so wonderfully filled with the Spirit and lived such victorious lives after they were saved.

1. These Christians Were Not Communists; the Bible Does Not Teach Communism

There are many striking differences between these New Testament Christians at Jerusalem about whom we are told, and communists. These people were devoted Christians, believers in Christ as their own Saviour and committed to follow Him until death. Communists are atheists, Christrejectors and Christ-haters. Another difference is that here there was no dictatorship. Here there was no seizing of property, no compulsion whatever. In communism it is just the opposite. Stalin and Lenin were bank robbers. The Russian Soviet "Republics" were founded on murder, assassination, confiscation, blood purges, and everything contrary to law and morality and Christianity. No well-informed person, then, could give this Scripture as a model teaching communism.

As we read the story here and follow on through the book

of Acts we find that there was a great emergency at Jerusalem. Thousands were saved. Of course there was great opposition. Many lost their means of livelihood. And these new Christians, fired with holy zeal for God and with earnest love for each other, gladly gave up their possessions and divided up their means to other Christians who were in need. It was an emergency and not an ordinary occasion. And the choice was entirely voluntary when anyone gave up his property. It must be remembered that the Bible nowhere commands people to give up all their property to the church or to the support of other Christians, and certainly it does not command one to give up property to the state. In fact, in this same church at Jerusalem when Ananias later sold his property and pretended to give all his means to God but withheld some, Peter said to him: "Why hast Satan filled thine heart to lie to the Holy Ghost, and to keep back part of the price of the land? Whiles it remained, was it not thine own? and after it was sold, was it not in thine own power? why hast thou conceived this thing in thine heart? thou hast not lied unto men, but unto God" (Acts 5:3, 4).

Ananias had a right to keep his property. He had not been commanded to sell it. When he sold it he had a right to keep the money. He had not been commanded to give it. His sin was in *pretending* to give everything when he did not; he lied instead of telling the truth. He sought honor and gave to please men and pretended to give what he did not give. His insincerity, his falsehood before God was the terrible sin. But Peter told him plainly that he could have kept the property or could have kept all the money, and it would not have been forbidden.

Later there was such a terrible famine and depression and want in Jerusalem among the Christians that Paul went to many churches collecting money and bringing it back to these saints at Jerusalem for the support of the poor (Acts 11:27-30). The great poverty at Jerusalem following Pentecost required heroic measures, and these earnest Christians gladly gave all for the Lord and for other Christians. However, even then the division of food caused distress and criticism (Acts 6:1), and the plan of everyone giving all of his property was abandoned at Jerusalem later and was never taken up in the other places where Christian churches were formed. But everywhere in the New Testament young Christians were taught to put God first in their money problems, and that was much of the secret of their happiness and prosperity and of God's wonderful care and provision for them. Oh, young Christian, you can learn from these Jerusalem converts!

2. Spirit-Filled Christianity Makes a Revolutionary Change in Attitude About Property!

Jews are thrifty people. Everybody ought to be thrifty. Jews on the average lay up carefully for their old age, they get their children well started in business, they ofteh take care of their own poor. This is an admirable quality. But wonderfully, these Jewish converts at Jerusalem had an entire change of attitude. They did not worry about tomorrow. They simply trusted the Lord about everything. They gave their property into His hands.

And that is exactly what the Lord Jesus, in Matthew 6: 25-34, teaches us to do. In that remarkable passage Jesus said:

"Therefore I say unto you, Take no thought for your life, what ye shall eat, or what ye shall drink; nor yet for your body, what ye shall put on. Is not the life more than meat, and the body than raiment? Behold the fowls of the air: for they sow not, neither do they reap, nor gather into barns; yet your heavenly Father feedeth them. Are ye not much better than they? Which of you by taking thought can add one cubit unto his stature? And why take ye thought for raiment? Consider the lilies of the field, how they grow; they toil not, neither to they spin: And yet I say unto you, That even Solomon in all his glory was not arrayed like one of these. Wherefore, if God so clothe the grass of the field, which to day is, and to morrow is cast into the oven, shall he not much more clothe you, O ye of little faith? Therefore take no thought, saying, What shall we eat? or, What shall we drink? or, Wherewithal shall we be clothed? (For after all these things do the Gentiles seek:) for your heavenly Father knoweth that ye have need of all these things. But seek ye first the kingdom of God, and his righteousness; and all these things shall be added unto you. Take therefore no thought for the morrow: for the morrow shall take thought

for the things of itself. Sufficient unto the day is the evil thereof."

A Christian is not to worry about his food. If he puts God first, the Lord will provide. He is not to worry about clothes. God feeds the fowls of the air and God clothes the lilies of the field. The God who takes care of His flowers and birds will take care of a Christian who trusts Him. Those who fret about the future and try to save lots of money and lay by in store for the future are of little faith, Jesus said. The Gentiles, heathen, unconverted people, are burdened about laying up money, having property, saving for the future. But a Christian has a better rule than that. Jesus said, "But seek ye first the kingdom of God, and his righteousness; and all these things shall be added unto you" (vs. 33).

That is the instruction of the Lord Jesus about property. And that is the way these New Testament Christians at Jerusalem felt. What a joy to be done with worry and fret about financial matters, just to labor and give and trust! I am sure they worked as hard as before, or harder. A good Christian makes a better workman than one who is not a good Christian. A good Christian will do more work in a day, will please his master better, will look after the welfare of his employer more than one who is not saved. The right kind of brotherly love will make Christians into good workmen and good businessmen. Thank God for the freedom from care and worry which comes when a Christian turns his financial affairs over to the Lord and depends upon God to provide, depends upon God to give him food and clothes and to care for his family so he is not afraid to give liberally to God's cause.

Is it not a shame that many a Christian is saved but has not had his attitude about money converted?

It is said that a number of new converts were being baptized once in a river, and a friend called to one man, saying, "Hey, Bill! You still have your billfold in your pocket. Do you want me to keep it for you?"

"No!" he replied. "I want that baptized, too!"

Of course it would do no good to baptize a pocketbook, literally, but certainly when a Christian gives himself to God, lays himself wholly on the altar, sets out to count himself dead to the old life and raised up to live a new life in Christ, it will mean that he will have an entirely different attitude toward money. Every good Christian who sets out to live by the blessed principles of success given here will have a Christian attitude toward his property.

3. Should a Christian Tithe?

Some people say that tithing is an Old Testament law, perhaps that it is ceremonial law, and that it was for Jews only under the ceremonial law. But in that they are mistaken. It is true that it is Leviticus 27:30 that says, "And all the tithe . . . is the Lord's: it is holy unto the Lord." But does it seem likely that a Jew under ceremonial law would need to acknowledge that he belonged to God and the tithe belonged to God, and a Christian, under grace, would feel no obligation to please God about his possessions? How strange that God should not claim the tithe of the Christian's income when He claimed the tithe of the Jews under the Mosaic ceremonial law! Actually, the tithe did not begin with the ceremonial law. Abraham gave tithes to Melchizedek (Gen. 14:17-20) long years before Moses was born and before the law was given at Mount Sinai; before there was a Hebrew nation. So the tithe did not originate with the Mosaic law. Hebrews, chapter 7, in the New Testament, tells us that Abraham in giving tithes to Melchizedek was a type of Christians giving tithes to Christ. Melchizedek was a type of Christ, and so, runs the divinely-given argument, the new covenant with Christ, represented by Abraham giving tithes to Melchizedek, is far superior to the old covenant wherein Jews under the law gave tithes to the Aaronic priesthood. Certainly Christians, then, would do well to follow this divinely-approved pattern.

In fact, the Lord Jesus spoke to the Pharisees in Matthew 23:23 and said, "Woe unto you, scribes and Pharisees, hypocrites! for ye pay tithe of mint and anise and cummin, and have omitted the weightier matters of the law, judgment, mercy, and faith: these ought ye to have done, and not to leave the other undone." The dear Lord Jesus called the Pharisees "hypocrites," not because they paid tithe even of the mint and anise and cummin, the little spices that grew in their gardens. No, He said, "These ought ye to have done"! They ought to have tithed. That was right. But He called them hypocrites because they left undone the weightier matters of the law, judgment, mercy and faith.

When Jesus said, "These ought ye to have done" about tithing, a Christian of course finds it easy to do.

In I Corinthians 16:2 we find proportionate giving taught in the New Testament. There Paul said, "Upon the first day of the week let every one of you lay by him in store, as God hath prospered him, that there be no gatherings when I come." They should lay by in store, each one, in proportion "as God hath prospered him." Now what percentage, what proportion do you think these New Testament Christians were expected to take out and lay by for the Lord? Certainly not less than the tenth. The inference is, it seems to me, that these people already knew what they should do, and they were encouraged to do it weekly. They should take out a proportionate part, and I have no doubt that they all understood it should be not less than a tenth. You see, all the preaching of the apostles and New Testament preachers was done out of the Old Testament. The New Testament was not yet written. People were familiar with the Old Testament before the New Testament was collected, and of course they would know what proportion in giving was customary.

It is an Old Testament Scripture that says, "Bring ye all the tithes into the storehouse . . ." (Mal. 3:10). But do you think God would ask less love, less faith and less cheerful giving from a New Testament Christian than from a Jew under the law? That does not seem reasonable.

If there is any difference in the teaching of the Old Testament and the New Testament on this question, the difference is that the New Testament always stresses that not only one tenth but the other nine-tenths, also, belong to God! I should bring tithes and offerings to the Lord, but I should remember that all the rest I have belongs to God just the same. Not a dime should be spent for anything except as we believe it will please God.

Why do you suppose God set a definite percentage, ten per cent, as the minimum of giving? I think that God intended this to be something like rent. If you live in a man's house and pay him rent, that is an acknowledgment of his ownership and that he has a right to demand possession of the house any time he is not pleased with you as a renter. When you borrow a man's money you pay him interest on the money. That is a token that the money belongs to him, must be paid back to him and that he must be given a strict accounting of the money that is borrowed. So when a Christian gives God tithes and offerings he simply means, "Dear Lord, I recognize that all I have belongs to You. When I bring You a part of what You have given me, it simply acknowledges that all belongs to You and I'll try to use it all for Your glory. This is a token of rent, or a token of interest on Your money, or an acknowledgment of Your ownership of me and all that I have!"

Should a Christian be content with giving exactly a tithe? By no means! Remember that in Malachi 3:8, 9 the Lord said to Israel: "Will a man rob God? Yet ye have robbed me. But ye say, Wherein have we robbed thee? In tithes and offerings. Ye are cursed with a curse: for ye have robbed me, even this whole nation." Those who did not bring God the tithe robbed Him; and those who did not bring offerings also robbed God. You see, God has a right to more than the exact one-tenth.

Tithing should not be a matter of bondage. It is a matter of grace and not law. That means that a Christian ought to give cheerfully and lovingly, more and more as God provides and makes it possible and as the urgency of the Lord's business and of getting out the gospel is felt in his heart.

I remember that I once carefully sought to give God exactly one penny out of every dime, one dime out of every dollar; and I kept books on it. But one day I felt ashamed that I was so strictly watching God as if I feared He would get more than He deserved. I threw away my account book and adopted the simpler plan of taking out the Lord's part once every week, or whenever the money came in. And my dear wife and I set out to give God at that time about twenty per cent, or more, and since that time He has helped us to be very, very happy in our giving. It has never been a burden, but a joy, and sometimes we gave literally all that came in beside the barest necessities.

4. Here Is a Christian's Promise of Material Prosperity and Daily Provision

In this little book I have been trying to lay on your heart

ways to be happy Christians, principles upon which you will be soul winners, will have your prayers answered, will have daily victory over sin and will be spiritually prosperous. I know there is great spiritual prosperity, great spiritual growth in grace in the matter of regular, liberal, conscientious and faithful giving to God's cause. But on this matter a Christian has a promise of more than spiritual blessing; he is promised material blessings, too.

Somebody says, "One should not give in order to be prospered." Well, perhaps that is not the highest motive for giving. One should love the Lord and be glad to do whatever He says. But the Bible gives this as a motive for giving! Again and again the Bible makes the plain offer and promise that one who gives according to the plan outlined in the Bible will find his needs met and he will be blessed.

Consider the following great promise:

"Bring ye all the tithes into the storehouse, that there may be meat in mine house, and prove me now herewith, saith the Lord of hosts, if I will not open you the windows of heaven, and pour you out a blessing, that there shall not be room enough to receive it."—Mal. 3:10.

This blessed promise is that material prosperity would come because Jews brought the tithes into the storehouse. It is material prosperity God speaks about here, for the next verse plainly says, "I will rebuke the devourer for your sakes, and he shall not destroy the fruits of your ground; neither shall your vine cast her fruit before the time in the field, saith the Lord of hosts" (Mal. 3:11).

The New Testament equally has explicit promises. In Luke 6:38 Jesus said:

"Give, and it shall be given unto you; good measure, pressed down, and shaken together, and running over, shall men give into your bosom. For with the same measure that ye mete withal it shall be measured to you again."

One cannot avoid the plain meaning here. According to the way a Christian gives, it is given to him. God sees that men will supply his needs as he gives. The way one receives is in proportion to the way one gives. Every Christian can trust the word of the Lord Jesus Christ about that.

Again, in II Corinthians 9:6-8, Paul the apostle by divine inspiration writes to the church at Corinth:

"But this I say, He which soweth sparingly shall reap also sparingly; and he which soweth bountifully shall reap also bountifully. Every man according as he purposeth in his heart, so let him give; not grudgingly, or of necessity: for God loveth a cheerful giver. And God is able to make all grace abound toward you; that ye, always having all sufficiency in all things, may abound to every good work."

Do you see the argument that God gives us here? The chapter starts with an explanation that Paul is talking about the offering for the saints at Jerusalem. And now he is sending others to collect the bounty of these saints at Corinth, and says, "He which soweth sparingly shall reap also sparingly; and he which soweth bountifully shall reap also bountifully." When one gives to God he is sowing. He will reap according to the way he sows! If he gives liberally, he will be prospered liberally. If he gives stingily, or sparingly, he will be prospered less. So is the clear statement of the Word of God.

To be sure, God wants the giving to come from the heart. He says, "Every man according as he purposeth in his heart, so let him give; not grudgingly, or of necessity: for God loveth a cheerful giver."

Oh, I would like to be so cheerful, so trusting, so joyful in my giving that the dear Lord would love me more because of my cheery and happy giving!

And verse 8 tells us frankly that God is able to supply all sufficiency in all things, and we ought to give with that in mind.

Oh, how many times I have proved for myself that when I put God first in money matters He supplies my needs. I wish I could tell you a hundred incidents to prove from my daily experiences that God cares for those who trust Him and put Him first in their giving.

I remember that in 1926 I gave up the pastorate of the First Baptist Church of Shamrock, Texas. I felt clearly led of God to go into the work of an evangelist. We had a new church building, a new pastor's home; the church had doubled in membership in two years. The Lord had wonderfully blessed and the people pleaded with me to remain. But I felt the urge and burning in my soul to go out into wider fields of soul winning in revival campaigns. So Mrs. Rice and

I talked and prayed about the matter. We decided to give up our $10,000 life insurance which I had taken out with the government when I was a soldier in World War I. We decided not to have a regular salary from that time forth. I do not think insurance is necessarily wrong. Each one will have to decide that for himself. God simply showed me that if I would trust Him wholly on this matter He would provide. I do not think that for a pastor to have a salary is wrong, although when I was pastor later I did not take a salary. God simply showed me that the more I would trust Him on this matter, the better He would take care of me. So we went out by faith. I had a holy covenant with God. "Lord," I said, "I'll take care of Your business, and You take care of mine!" Oh, how well God has cared for my business! I only wish I had cared for His business one-half as well!

Raising a big family of girls, paying for music lessons, paying college tuition, paying thousands of dollars for radio time, paying for the publication of books and pamphlets by the million, paying the deficit on the weekly paper, THE SWORD OF THE LORD, year after year—how well I had a chance to try God out and to see if He would give as I gave, if when I sowed bountifully I would reap bountifully. And I found it works!

Dear Christian, you cannot beat God at giving! The more you give from an honest, loving, trusting heart, the more God will see that you are prospered even in daily provision and in financial matters. So this is certainly an important principle upon which a Christian should build his life if he hopes to be a happy Christian, a successful Christian; if he hopes to have his prayers answered and to have his daily needs provided. God's people do not need to be helpless nor left orphans and unprovided for. If you seek first the kingdom of God and sow bountifully, you will reap bountifully even in material things. God's promises say so and millions of Christians who have tried it prove the point!

5. Some Suggestions About How to Give

I believe that the following suggestions will help a young Christian to get started to giving in a way that will please God.

First, it seems to me wisest for most Christians simply to

take out the Lord's part of the income each week. That is the plan given in I Corinthians 16:2, "Upon the first day of the week let every one of you lay by him in store, as God has prospered . . ."

For those who get paid by the day or by the week, certainly this is the ideal plan. You may take the tithe and any freewill offerings you feel led to give out of the income and put it in a safe place to be given later, for the Lord. Some people like to give the full tithe every Sunday, and that is all right, though the Scripture does not command that the money all be given at one time. The command is simply to "lay by him in store." One should put the Lord's money in a separate place. It may be put in a separate bank account, or put in a safe place about the home, or it may all be given at once; but the Lord's part should be taken out once a week where the income is daily or weekly.

Let me earnestly suggest that every Christian take the Lord's part out *first*. God should be first in our plans. In the Old Testament ceremonial law God required that "the firstling of the flock" should be given to Him. The prophet Elijah, in a terrible time of drought, was fed by a widow of Zarephath. She had only a handful of meal in a barrel and a little oil in a cruse, and was gathering two sticks to make a fire and cook her last little pitiful cake before she and her son died. But Elijah said, "Fear not; go and do as thou hast said: but make me thereof a little cake first, and bring it unto me, and after make for thee and for thy son. For thus saith the Lord God of Israel, The barrel of meal shall not waste, neither shall the cruse of oil fail, until the day that the Lord sendeth rain upon the earth" (I Kings 17:13, 14). And as certain as God's promise, so certain was His doing. The widow made first a little cake for the prophet of God and God then increased the meal and oil enough to feed her and her son until the famine was over! Oh, take the Lord's part out first as a token of your full surrender and your faith, because you really want to put God first in your heart.

Do you run a business? Do you own a store or laundry or farm or manufacturing plant? If you take for yourself a regular salary, you would simply tithe the salary. Otherwise, you would not tithe the total gross income, but only the income after supplies were paid for, after the rent was paid and other expenses necessary in running the business. Of course I do not mean you should deduct your own personal expenses or your family's expenses. One who owns a grocery store, for example, would first pay for the groceries bought and pay rent on the building, taxes and upkeep on the building, and pay his store help, heat, lights and gas; and then out of the money left, net profit, he would give tithes and offerings.

Perhaps one on a farm would wonder whether to tithe all the increase on the farm or to take out the money spent for actual farming operations, the money for seed, the feed bought for cattle, etc. It seems to have been the custom among the Jews to give tithes of all the increase of the land. If one desires to first pay for the seed used, the feed bought, machinery bought, and hired labor, that would be all right; but in that case one would need to charge himself so much rent, charge himself for garden vegetables, eggs, pork and other provisions which were supplied him by the farm. It is much simpler for a farmer living on a home farm to simply give a tenth of all the crops, a tenth of the cattle, a tenth of the chickens, eggs, etc. What he might spend for seed or feed or machinery would thus be overbalanced by his own free rent and for much of the food he would get from the farm on which he would not otherwise pay a tithe.

Shall a Christian give all his tithes through his local church treasury and allow the church board to decide how the money shall be spent? Usually not, I should think. Remember that the Scripture says, "All the tithe . . . is the Lord's." It does not say, "All the tithe is the church's." The tithe does not belong to the pastor, does not belong to the church, does not belong to the denominational headquarters. The tithe belongs to the Lord. And you are the Lord's steward, which means that when God puts money in your hand, you must account to God for the way it is used and where your gifts go.

Usually it is certainly right for a Christian to give money through the local church. Every church member properly feels a burden to help support his own pastor, to help take care of the house of God, to support the missionary program of the church. If one is a member of a church where he cannot honestly put his money, it is doubtful whether he ought to

put his influence and his presence there. I think every
Christian who is in a Bible-believing church should have a
regular, definite part in the church's financial program and
should do it cheerfully and, as far as possible, in ways pleasing to the church leaders.

However, it is clearly implied in the Bible that the Christian himself must decide where he gives and how he gives,
"every man as he purposeth in his heart." For example, in
I Corinthians 16:2 Paul expressly commanded that each
Christian should lay aside a proportionate part of his income
and keep it until Paul should come to take it with him for the
poor saints at Jerusalem. In that case there is no evidence
that the money necessarily would go through the church
treasury at all. The individual Christian would save up the
money and turn it over to Paul. Possibly they all brought it
and put it in a common fund, and the church may have turned it all over to Paul together. That we do not know. But the
Scripture mentioned certainly does not teach that all the
money has to go through the local church treasury.

Malachi 3:10 says, "Bring ye all the tithes into the storehouse, that there may be meat in mine house . . ." The
storehouse there mentioned was the temple in the Old Testament. The work to be supported for the whole nation was the
support of the priests and Levites at the temple. In that case
the tithes were all to be brought to Jerusalem. But the New
Testament does not teach that the church treasury takes the
place of the temple treasury.

Many of the finest soul-winning works go on without the
official backing of denominations. Dr. Charles E. Fuller, Dr.
Walter Maier, and other great radio preachers carry on their
work at tremendous cost, supported by Bible-believing Christians. I believe God has blessed these works and wants them
to continue. Very little of the offerings to support these
works come in through church treasuries. The great faith
missions, such as the China Inland Mission, the Sudan In-
terior Mission, and the Central American Mission, receive
their support largely outside of denominational headquarters
and local church treasuries, as I understand it. I believe God
wants these works to continue and wants them supported by
people who give in Jesus' name.

And that leads me to say that giving without praying and

without earnest consideration could not please God. Ask the Lord what He wants you to do with His money! Pray definitely that God will use it to win souls. Pray that He will help you to give more for His glory!

And of course the tithe must be used to honor Jesus Christ. It is His money, not yours. It must be used to His glory. And we know the thing closest to His heart is the saving of sinners. So set out to be a happy, prosperous Christian by putting God first in all your possessions. And how wonderfully He will prove Himself to you!

CHAPTER VII

SOUL WINNING

Seventh Secret of Christian Happiness and Prosperity

WE SOMETIMES SPEAK of "the revival at Pentecost." Actually, the revival did not end at Pentecost. We are told, "And they, continuing daily with one accord in the temple, and breaking bread from house to house, did eat their meat with gladness and singleness of heart, Praising God, and having favour with all the people. And the Lord added to the church daily such as should be saved" (Acts 2:46, 47).

People were added to the church daily! And I think this means the local congregation.

1. How New Testament Christians Won Souls

Some churches these days receive new converts into the church once a year, at Easter time. Other churches have a membership committee that meets once a month, and once a month new converts, if any, may be received into the church. When I was a pastor we regularly received members each week and it was a very, very unusual Sunday in which there were not converts coming for baptism on profession of their faith in Christ and for membership in the church. But this wonderful revival church in Jerusalem received members every day! "The Lord added to the church daily such as should be saved."

Ah, there is the purpose of a church! These people knew what God intended churches for! The Lord Jesus left us here to win souls. He has given to us the Great Commission to take the gospel to every creature. He told the apostles that they should go out and make disciples of all nations and that the new converts, when baptized, should be taught "to observe all things whatsoever I have commanded you" (Matt. 28:20). Every convert at Jerusalem had the instructions to carry out the Great Commission just as Jesus gave it to the apostles. So these wonderfully happy, Spirit-filled Christians kept on winning souls and daily God added to the church the new converts. That is the seventh great principle of happiness and prosperity for a Christian life: soul winning.

And these converts kept it up! In Acts 4:4 we are told, "Howbeit many of them which heard the word believed; and the number of the men was about five thousand." There were five thousand men in that church, besides the women and children! And Acts 4:33 says, "And with great power gave the apostles witness of the resurrection of the Lord Jesus: and great grace was upon them all." Acts 5:14 says, "And believers were the more added to the Lord, multitudes both of men and women." Acts 5:42 tells us, "And daily in the temple, and in every house, they ceased not to teach and preach Jesus Christ."

Oh, for Christians who carry on the work of a revival like that, daily winning souls, carrying on the blessing to everybody about them! That is what new converts, as well as older Christians, are supposed to do.

2. Soul Winning, the Dearest Thing on Earth to Jesus!

I wonder, dear Christian, do you remember the main thing on the heart of Jesus Christ? Do you not know how He gave Himself to leave Heaven, to live among the poorest of people, and then to be abused and hated? Do you remember that Jesus suffered the torments in Gethsemane, sweat the bloody sweat in an agony of soul, and then was kissed with a traitor's kiss and led away to be tried? Do you remember the crown of thorns they put on His head and how they spit in His face and plucked out His beard? Do you remember how they bound His hands and feet, tore off His garments and beat Him with a Roman scourge, the cat-o'-nine-tails? Do you remember how they laid upon Him the heavy cross, how He stumbled along the road to Calvary with it until He fell; then how He was nailed to that cross and then it was lifted up to hold Him there six hours until He died? Do you remember that even God the Father turned His face away from Jesus and He prayed, "My God, my God, why has thou forsaken me"? Do you remember the three hours of darkness and then that He gave up the ghost? And, dear friend, remember that all this was to keep souls out of Hell! The third day He arose again from the grave, to be our justification. He ascended up to the Father and there He is today, our High Priest, interceding for us. Oh, dear Christian, we know what Jesus wants; He wants souls saved! He Himself told us, "Likewise joy shall be in heaven over one sinner that repenteth, more than over ninety and nine just persons, which need no repentance" (Luke 15:7).

How can God be pleased with any Christian who is baptized and joins the church and reads his Bible and gives his money and prays, but will not do the main thing that Jesus wants people to do? Oh, this is the crowning climax of a happy, prosperous Christian life, to win souls! There is no happiness that I know anything about that can compare with a soul winner's joy. You remember that Psalm 126:5, 6 says, "They that sow in tears shall reap in joy. He that goeth forth and weepeth, bearing precious seed, shall doubtless come again with rejoicing, bringing his sheaves with him." I know what it is to sow in tears; but, thank God, I know what it is to reap in joy, too! I know what it is to go forth weeping; but, oh, praise the Lord, I know what it means to come back rejoicing with sheaves! If you ever really get this blessing of soul winning and get a habit of soul winning you will have the highest kind of joy of which a Christian is capable in this world. And you will know that one day when you meet Jesus, He will be pleased. You will know in Heaven you will have a rich reward, for Daniel 12:3 says, "They that be wise shall shine as the brightness of the firmament; and they that turn many to righteousness as the stars for ever and ever."

Even a new convert can do it. How well I remember when I was fifteen years old and won my first convert, a boy about fourteen. Thank God, he was happy about it, too! I never shall forget how he loved me. One day after both of us were men I went back to that little cow town where I grew up, to preach, and a tall, strong man came to me and said, "John, do you remember me?"

I said, "Albert, is it you?"

What a glad meeting it was! Then he brought in his wife and children to meet me, the man who had won him to Christ when I was fifteen years old and he was about fourteen.

3. Some Suggestions About How to Win Souls

Here are some suggestions about how to do it.

First, use the Word of God. You should set out to memorize some verses of Scripture so that you can tell people how to be saved and why they need to be saved, and settle their doubts. I suggest that you read carefully, over and over, my little pamphlet, *"What Must I Do to Be Saved?"* As you read it, note the Scriptures, then look them up in your Bible, mark them there and memorize them. There you will find many, many Scriptures that show people they are sinners, that show them good works will not save and that show them how to trust in Jesus Christ. Then perhaps you might like to get Dr. R. A. Torrey's *Vest Pocket Companion for Soul Winners*. It has 118 pages with collections of Scriptures for every use of the soul winner. If you will have this at hand for a time until you learn it and grow familiar with it, it will help you to win souls. But remember that it is wiser to read directly out of the Bible itself and show sinners what God's Word really says. After you learn where the soul-winning promises are and what they say, use the Bible itself as far as possible.

Second, make your soul winning a matter of earnest prayer. You know that if you are to be a soul winner the Holy Spirit must come upon you, must fill you, must teach you what to say. The Holy Spirit must convict sinners when you speak to them if they are going to be convicted. So spend much time in prayer for sinners, asking particularly that the Spirit of God will guide you and give you power as you work for Him.

Third, I suggest that, where that is possible, you get sinners out to church to hear some gospel preacher, some soul-winning evangelist or pastor. If you talk to them about Christ ahead of time and sit with them in the service, you may often encourage them by simply offering to walk down to the front with them, or to an inquiry room. Or you may ask such a friend to go with you to meet the pastor after the service, and frankly tell the pastor in his presence, "Here is a friend of mine I want you to meet; I am praying for him that he may be saved." God will help you. Many young and inexperienced Christians have been able to win souls by co-operating with the pastor or the evangelist in the public services.

Fourth, press for real decision. Just talking in general terms is not enough. No salesman is a good salesman who does not get names signed on the dotted line, who does not get actual orders. So urge upon sinners to accept Christ and pray that God will give you definite results day by day.

Last of all, you cannot expect to win many souls unless you go after them wherever they are. Ask God to give you boldness. Ask the Spirit of God to show you where to go and what to say. And if He guides you He will help you to find the key to hungry hearts. He can help you to get in touch with people who need the gospel. Talk with men where you work. Talk with other students with you in school. When you meet people it is often an easy matter, if you are kindly and if you show yourself to be a genuine friend, to find out whether or not they know the Lord Jesus. It takes an earnest heart and genuine sincerity, and also it takes lots of work. So go after sinners, and may God give you wisdom and grace. May God give you a burning heart and a loving heart as you win souls to Jesus Christ.

When you win a soul, then of course you should try to see that that new convert learns the lessons you are learning in this book so he, too, can follow the Great Commission and be a successful and happy Christian and be a soul winner. So take time to see that one converted has assurance of salvation by the Word of God, to see that the new converts are enlisted in attending church, in reading the Bible and in regular prayer habits.

A Closing Word

The matters discussed in this book are so important that

I urge every reader to plan to go through the entire book again, reading it carefully and prayerfully, and set out to check your life habits and plans by those followed by the Christians at Jerusalem, about whom we have studied. Then if you really follow these plans I know you will be a happy, prosperous Christian with the blessing of God upon you, with great joy in your heart, and with much fruit to present to the Saviour who died for you. God bless you as you set out to be a prosperous, happy, successful Christian!

Will you help to spread this little book? Wherever possible, a copy should go to every new convert. And if there are ways in which I can help you, please feel free to write the author.

DR. JOHN R. RICE

P. O. Box 1099

Murfreesboro, Tennessee

37130